ArcView

GIS
means
Business

Christian Harder

ENVIRONMENTAL SYSTEMS RESEARCH INSTITUTE, INC.

PUBLISHED BY
Environmental Systems Research Institute, Inc.
380 New York Street
Redlands, California 92373-8100

Environmental Systems Research Institute, Inc.
 ArcView GIS Means Business
 ISBN 1-879102-51-X

ArcView uses Neuron Data's Open Interface.

Contents

Contents

Environmental Systems Research Institute, Inc.

Contents

Environmental Systems Research Institute, Inc.

Preface

Geographic information systems (GIS) are reshaping the business world. From multinational corporations to entrepreneurial start-ups, from hardware stores to hospitals, companies of every kind are bringing geographic analysis to bear on their business problems. In the process, they're making better decisions, better serving their customers, and finding new and better market opportunities.

Although GIS has been evolving for thirty years (that is to say, it's a mature technology), only in the past five years has it begun to take hold in the private sector. The development of powerful personal computers, coupled with easy-to-use GIS products and widely available data, has created a new breed of GIS practitioner: the business professional.

This book presents ten success stories that chronicle different applications of GIS technology to a variety of common business problems. These stories only hint at the vast potential of GIS in business.

The accompanying CD–ROM contains a trial copy of ArcView® GIS software (the software package from ESRI featured in the book), along with a comprehensive online tutorial. Don't worry: you don't need to load or learn anything to read the book. The case studies are presented in ordinary language that explains how GIS analysis solves business problems; no prior technical knowledge is assumed. Our hope is simply that once you see the benefits GIS has to offer, you'll be interested in knowing more about how it works. At that point, the CD will be a good place to start.

Acknowledgments

This book could not have been written were it not for the cooperation of the ArcView GIS users who shared their experiences (and trusted me with their data and projects). You'll find them all acknowledged by name at the end of each of the case studies.

A number of people at ESRI also played significant roles in producing this book.

Tim Ormsby and Michael Karman edited numerous drafts and suggested many ways to tell the stories without burying the reader in overly technical language. Michael Hyatt designed the book and copyedited the final manuscript. Gina Davidson came through with a fine cover design, and did so under deadline.

Damian Spangrud, Jim McAbee, and Matt McGunigle patiently answered many technical questions related to ArcView GIS.

In the early stages of development, Dan Bellas, Drew Bieber, Dave LaShell, Bob Ruschman, and Scott Royer all helped identify successful ArcView GIS users who were willing to go on the record.

Dr. Michael Phoenix, Steve Trammell, Tony Burns, and Eileen Napoleon of ESRI, and Dr. Jim Spee of the University of Redlands, all took the time to review early drafts of the manuscript and suggest useful changes.

Pat Breslin, Ron Gullon, and Randy Worch created the companion CD–ROM.

And finally, thanks to Bill Miller and Judy Boyd, who believed in the project from the start and provided the resources needed to make it happen, and to Jack Dangermond, for creating an organization like ESRI, where people with ideas are encouraged to see them through.

CHAPTER 1

GIS in business

Geographic information systems (GIS) are changing the landscape of business. Once the tool of geographers and cartographers, GIS has moved from the research center to the corporate cubicle, from the scientist's workstation to the businessman's personal computer, from the mapmaker to the manager. In the process, it has grown into a major industry employing tens of thousands of people. In 1996, the worldwide market for GIS software, hardware, and services topped $6 billion in revenue.

GIS at work

Business managers, marketing strategists, financial analysts, and professional planners are increasingly relying on GIS to organize, analyze, and present their business data. By tying information to specific locations, like street addresses, ZIP Codes, and census tracts, they are creating "business maps" that help them identify patterns and understand relationships not apparent from tables and charts.

Whether they're scouting store locations, reorganizing sales territories, improving delivery routes, identifying new markets, or publishing maps on the Internet, these "spatially literate" users have learned to unleash the power of GIS in their businesses.

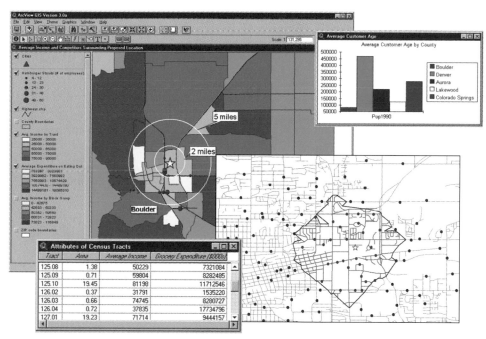

A fast-food franchisor uses GIS to analyze a possible new site (marked with a yellow star). Relevant factors include the average age and income of people in the surrounding area, the locations of major roads, and the proximity of competitors.

Real-world examples

The ten case studies in this book show you how a variety of real business-people have used ArcView® GIS software (desktop GIS software from Environmental Systems Research Institute, Inc.) to solve their business problems. These people didn't start off as geographers, or GIS experts—they simply rolled up their sleeves and learned how to make the software do what they needed.

The cases may or may not address the specific types of problems you face in your line of work, but chances are you'll see some familiar situations. And if that's true, it means you'll also see how GIS strategies can bring new solutions—and success—to your business.

If you already know about GIS and how it works, you may want to skip directly to the case studies. If not, it will be worth a few moments of your time to read the rest of this chapter. Welcome to a book in which maps are more than just your journey's blueprint—they are the journey itself.

Ace Hardware Corporation

THE PRESS-ENTERPRISE

REALTY ADVISORS

ESRI

SEA · KAYAKING

Ink Tech

CHASE

Providence/
St. Peter Hospital

Market researchers, business managers, and financial analysts at the companies featured in this book have discovered the power of ArcView GIS software to solve business problems.

Why geography matters

To most of us, geography is a tangle of dusty facts, like *The capital of New Zealand is Wellington* or *Death Valley is the lowest place in the Western Hemisphere.* Unless you're a game show contestant, it's hard to see the relevance of these tidbits of information. But suppose an acquaintance wants to sell you a roadside diner in the Mojave Desert. Are you interested? If you know that the diner is located on Interstate 15—the main thoroughfare between Southern California and Las Vegas—you just might be. If, on the other hand, it lies on a forsaken stretch of highway in the Sheep Hole Mountains, you'd tell the seller to take a hike. And it's in this sense—the sense in which knowing where things are is essential to rational decision making—that geography matters to business.

Fine—but isn't this just plain common sense? After all, it doesn't take a genius to put a hamburger stand next to a high school or a bait shop by a lake. But things aren't always that simple. Consider a couple of examples. After studying population and economic growth in the western United States, an airline adds direct flights to a handful of new cities and sees its numbers fly. In Texas, a department store, analyzing credit card receipts by ZIP Code, infers that a large number of its customers drive along a particular section of freeway to reach the mall—so the store makes some smart choices about where to place billboard ads. In cases like these, the business decisions are not at all obvious: what is clear, though, is that geographical considerations shaped the outcome.

Linking location to information (or bringing the *where* to bear on the *what*) is a process that applies to many aspects of business. Choosing a site, targeting a market, planning a distribution network or delivery route, drawing up sales territories, allocating resources—all these problems involve questions of geography. Where are my customers—actual and potential? In which neighborhoods or ZIP Code areas do consumers with the right profile live? Where will they be living five years from now? Where are my competitors located? Which areas might be underserved? Sometimes the questions are large in scope, and sometimes they're quite specific: how close is the nearest freeway exit? How far away is the airport or the waterfront? Which buildings are properly zoned, have affordable leases, and lie within a five-minute walk of the subway station?

GIS gives you the power to answer these and many other questions—quickly, accurately, and demonstrably. And that, in short, is what makes it such a valuable tool to your business. As you become familiar with the principles and techniques of geographic analysis, you'll find yourself asking (and answering) questions that wouldn't even have occurred to you before. And when that happens, you'll lead your business to higher ground.

What is GIS?

What is a geographic information system? There are probably as many definitions as there are applications for GIS. For the purposes of this book, a GIS is a particular kind of software program that runs on personal computers. In many ways it resembles a database program (it analyzes and relates information stored as records), but with one crucial difference: each record in a GIS database contains information used to draw a geometric shape—usually a point, a line, or a polygon.

That shape, in turn, represents a unique place on earth to which the data corresponds. In other words, a record in a GIS file describing Travis County, Texas, would include not only fields of text and numeric information (name, area, and so on), but also fields of *spatial data* enabling the computer to draw Travis County as a boundary of a certain size and shape. You can therefore think of a GIS as a spatial database—a database that stores the location and shape of information.

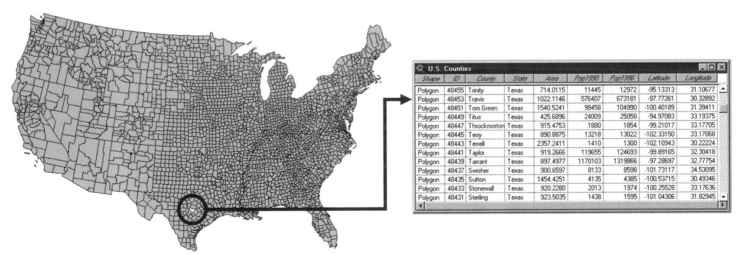

Shape	ID	County	State	Area	Pop1990	Pop1996	Latitude	Longitude
Polygon	48455	Trinity	Texas	714.0115	11445	12972	-95.13313	31.10677
Polygon	48453	Travis	Texas	1022.1146	576407	673181	-97.77261	30.32892
Polygon	48451	Tom Green	Texas	1540.5241	98458	104990	-100.40189	31.39411
Polygon	48449	Titus	Texas	425.6896	24009	25058	-94.97083	33.19375
Polygon	48447	Throckmorton	Texas	915.4753	1880	1854	-99.21017	33.17705
Polygon	48445	Terry	Texas	890.8875	13218	13022	-102.33150	33.17068
Polygon	48443	Terrell	Texas	2357.2411	1410	1300	-102.10943	30.22224
Polygon	48441	Taylor	Texas	919.2666	119655	124693	-99.89165	32.30418
Polygon	48439	Tarrant	Texas	897.4977	1170103	1319866	-97.28697	32.77754
Polygon	48437	Swisher	Texas	900.6597	8133	8598	-101.73117	34.53095
Polygon	48435	Sutton	Texas	1454.4251	4135	4385	-100.53715	30.49346
Polygon	48433	Stonewall	Texas	920.2280	2013	1974	-100.25528	33.17636
Polygon	48431	Sterling	Texas	923.5035	1438	1595	-101.04306	31.82945

Each record in this map file contains spatial information needed to draw a particular U.S. county. When the file is opened, the computer draws a complete county map of the United States.

But a GIS doesn't simply store and display information about places or physical features—it stores and displays information that can be *linked* to places; that is, information that has a geographical location. And, as it happens, that encompasses a great deal of information. The fact that two plus two equals four has nothing to do with geography (although it would if it were true in some places and false in others). The fact, on the other hand, that luxury cars are mostly bought by people who earn more than $100,000 a year does have a geographical aspect. So does the fact that a significant percentage of Hispanic people prefer to buy groceries with Spanish-language labeling or to shop in a store where Spanish is spoken. Those people live *somewhere*. And a GIS can show you where.

For this reason, a GIS is more than a computer system for drawing maps (although it does draw maps extremely well): it's really a system for mapping and analyzing the geographical distribution of data. And the data is any information you can store in a database, so long as it can be linked to a location.

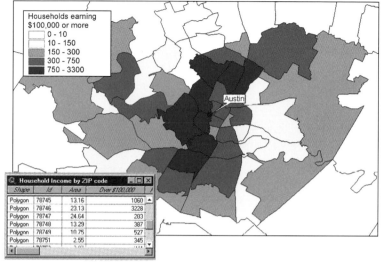

This map of household income in Travis County, Texas, shows the ZIP Codes with the most people earning over $100,000 a year. A luxury car dealer could target these ZIP Codes for marketing efforts.

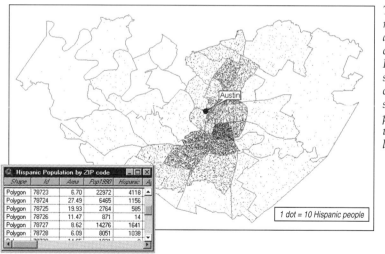

This dot density map of the same area shows concentrations of Hispanics. A supermarket chain catering to this segment of the population could use the map to help locate a new store.

GIS map files can represent the whole world or any part of it, in greater or lesser detail, by any of various subdivisions (political boundaries, postal codes, census designations, streets, and so on). They can represent all kinds of natural and man-made features as well: rivers, lakes, highways, hospitals, and so on. These map files are available from a variety of sources. Many come included with GIS packages; others can be obtained from both commercial vendors and government agencies. (You'll learn more about this in chapter 12, "Getting GIS data for business applications.") In addition, you can create your own map files from data (such as customer address lists) that is implicitly geographic. There are map files to represent almost any place with almost any kind of statistical information you might want. And because a GIS is a relational database, you can easily link your own existing data to an appropriate map file.

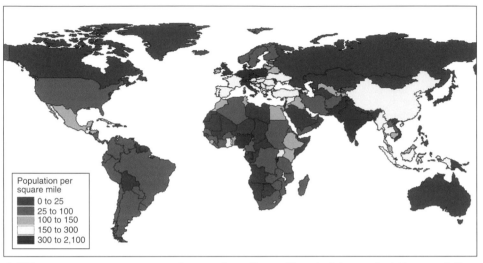

Population per square mile
- 0 to 25
- 25 to 100
- 100 to 150
- 150 to 300
- 300 to 2,100

A GIS map can represent an area as large as the entire world, as in this map depicting population density by country.

Assessed value
- Under $100,000
- $100,000 to $125,000
- $125,000 to $150,000
- $150,000 to $200,000
- Over $200,000

Or it can show an area as small as a neighborhood. This map displays the property values of land parcels in a section of San Jose, California.

Environmental Systems Research Institute, Inc.

The map paradigm

We often say "I see" to mean "I understand." Pattern recognition is something human beings excel at—that's why you know a Great Dane and a French Poodle are both dogs, despite their obvious differences, and that's why human scrutiny is still the best way to analyze satellite and aerial reconnaissance photos in an era of massive super-computing capability.

One of the great insights of GIS is that there is a vast difference between seeing data in a table of rows and columns (a display mode natural to computers and accountants) and seeing it presented in the form of a map. The difference is not simply aesthetic, it's conceptual—it turns out that the way you see your data has a profound effect on the connections you make and the conclusions you draw from it.

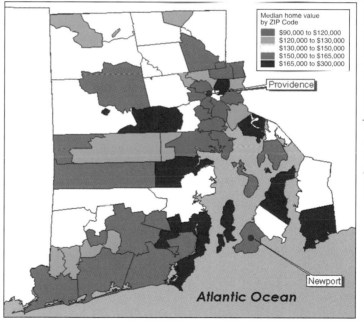

The table and the map both show the same data: the median value of homes by ZIP Code in Rhode Island. But even for someone familiar with the state's geography, the table has limited value as a tool for understanding the housing market. By contrast, the information on the map is easy to grasp, even for a person who's never been to Rhode Island.

Zip	Pop1996	Post Office	Median home value
02861	26129	PAWTUCKET	111900
02863	17163	CENTRAL FALLS	102900
02864	28595	CUMBERLAND	143200
02865	14407	LINCOLN	156700
02871	16437	PORTSMOUTH	173300
02872	121	PRUDENCE ISLAND	156000
02874	3637	SAUNDERSTOWN	169500
02877	1139	SLOCUM	162800
02878	13745	TIVERTON	139600
02879	14374	WAKEFIELD	161500
02881	7565	KINGSTON	172300
02882	14383	NARRAGANSETT	168200
02883	1837	PEACE DALE	116800
02885	11462	WARREN	138100
02886	40875	WARWICK	116400
02888	20794	WARWICK	114500
02889	20702	WARWICK	114000
02891	21610	WESTERLY	155800
02892	4300	WEST KINGSTON	150500
02893	28126	WEST WARWICK	124300
02894	743	WOOD RIVER JUNCT	124200
02895	38452	WOONSOCKET	127300

Median home value by ZIP Code
- $90,000 to $120,000
- $120,000 to $130,000
- $130,000 to $150,000
- $150,000 to $165,000
- $165,000 to $300,000

Providence

Newport

Atlantic Ocean

GIS helps you visualize data

A GIS lets you visually represent the data in any field of a map file: as differing shades of color, as symbols of different sizes, as dot patterns of varying density, or in other ways. If you change the information in the file, the display is automatically updated. And if you have different map files representing features that occupy common geographic space, you can add multiple layers of data to the same display. This lets you create a map as rich in information as you want.

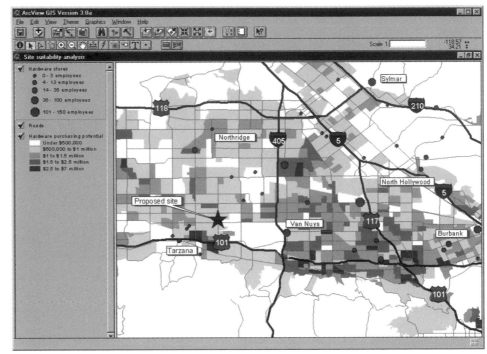

This map of the area around Van Nuys, California, contains multiple layers of spatial data, each from a separate data file. The entire area is shaded beige to red according to consumer purchasing power. City streets are shown as thin gray lines, while highways and interstates are thicker blue lines. Pink dots represent the locations of retail hardware stores; the size of each dot reflects the number of employees the store has. All the information in the map is relevant to a specific business problem: where to locate a new hardware store.

GIS helps you analyze data

As with any database, the greatest virtue of a GIS is its analytical power. A GIS has a full array of query tools: logical operators, math functions, a scripting language. The ability to display the results of your queries geographically is an advantage in itself, but GIS offers something much more important—the unique capacity to do spatial analysis, making it possible to ask and answer questions that are beyond the scope of traditional databases.

Suppose you have three stores and you want to compare the demographics around each to help understand why two are thriving and one is doing poorly. Using spatial analysis, you can calculate a demographic profile for all the households that lie within a fifteen-minute drive of each store. Or say you want to make sure your delivery driver is taking the most efficient route as he makes his rounds. With spatial analysis you can find the best route from your factory and give the driver turn-by-turn directions.

In the examples above, the maps are certainly useful, but it is the *information extracted* by spatial analysis that is most important. This information would either be impossible or extremely difficult to obtain without a GIS.

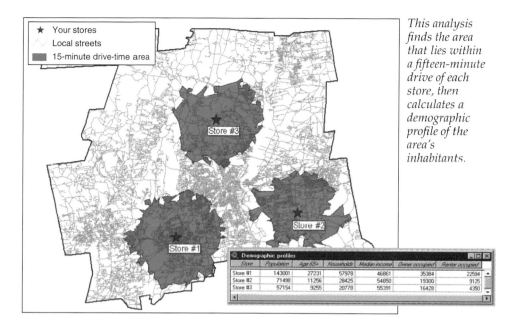

This analysis finds the area that lies within a fifteen-minute drive of each store, then calculates a demographic profile of the area's inhabitants.

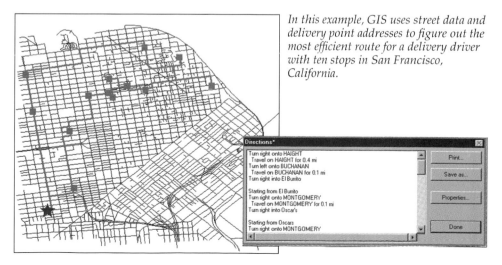

In this example, GIS uses street data and delivery point addresses to figure out the most efficient route for a delivery driver with ten stops in San Francisco, California.

GIS helps you present data

In business, it helps to see something that nobody else sees, but that in itself may not be enough. You have to be able to communicate what you know—whether you're dealing with your boss, a client, a management committee, or a roomful of shareholders. GIS gives you the layout and drawing tools that help you make your case (on paper or online) with clear, compelling documents.

GIS is also being employed as a multimedia technology—delivering digital audio and video information linked to maps, charts, and tables.

GIS and the Internet

On the Internet, interactive applications allow your customers to produce their own custom maps, twenty-four hours a day, anywhere in the world. Whether it's in helping people find the nearest automated teller machine, or showing a traveler all the Chinese restaurants within a mile of her hotel, maps delivered via the Internet are already changing the way businesses think of customer service.

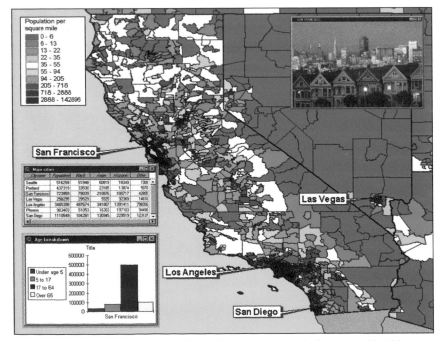

Interactive maps are increasingly being "published" on the Internet, like this popular ATM locator application developed for the Visa Corporation using ESRI's MapObjects™ embeddable mapping component technology.

GIS can integrate maps, charts, tables, and images in a single document, like this one depicting the demographics of California and Nevada.

ArcView GIS and ESRI

The case studies presented in this book use a wide range of GIS problem-solving methods and data from a variety of sources. What they all have in common is ArcView GIS software from Environmental Systems Research Institute, Inc. (Redlands, California).

ESRI is the world's largest company dedicated to GIS. ESRI® software, including ARC/INFO®, ArcView GIS, and MapObjects software, is used throughout the world.

The latest version of ArcView GIS represents the state of the art in this class of software. ArcView is by far the most functional GIS ever developed for the personal computer.

The case studies

Now that you've gotten your bearings, you're ready to proceed to the case studies. The intention throughout is to show you the kinds of problems that GIS can solve and the techniques used to solve them—not to belabor the details of how the software works. That experience lies down the road in your own GIS future.

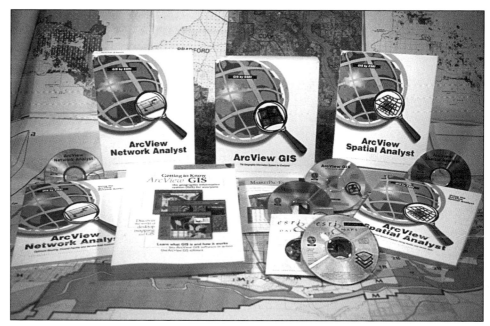

ArcView GIS *software is the core product in the expanding ArcView software family.*

Researching retail markets

The most successful retail marketers make it their business to know who their customers are and where they come from. Long before the arrival of computers, retailers depended on old-fashioned research—phone, mail, and in-store surveys—to gather information about their clientele. What has changed with computers is how that information is interpreted and used to make better marketing decisions.

In this chapter, you'll see how a national dealer-owned hardware cooperative uses ArcView GIS to help its retailers make sense of survey data collected in their stores. You'll then see how a store in Phoenix, Arizona, used this information to focus and redirect its advertising dollars.

Ace is the place

Ace Hardware Corporation (Oak Brook, Illinois) is one of the world's leading wholesale hardware cooperatives, with 1996 sales of over $2.7 billion. From its corporate headquarters near Chicago, the company exercises the combined buying power of over 5,000 independent Ace retailers around the globe.

These independent dealers compete successfully against the big warehouse-style superstores by offering high-quality, well-packaged products, accompanied by first-rate customer service.

In addition to providing the benefits of cooperative buying and national advertising, Ace Hardware Corporation lends its retailers considerable expertise in market research. Increasingly, this research is carried out with the help of GIS.

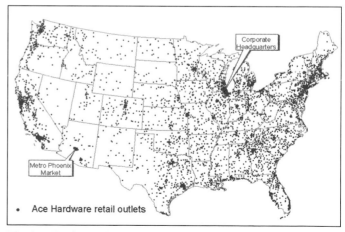

The Ace Hardware Corporation supports a worldwide network of over 5,000 independent retailers, including 4,800 stores in the continental United States.

The role of GIS

From the company's headquarters in Oak Brook, a team of marketing research specialists uses ArcView GIS to map and analyze research data for corporate management, field staff, and individual Ace retailers.

Top management relies on GIS to identify underserved regions and to compare various markets from a national perspective. Corporate departments responsible for conventions, merchandising, advertising, and human resources use maps and GIS analysis to solve a variety of problems, from deciding whether or not to accept new Ace retailer affiliations to targeting specific stores for relocation.

For local retailers, primary research (like in-store surveys) can often be given a revealing geographical interpretation. That was certainly the case in a customer survey research project conducted for the management of Paradise Valley Ace Hardware in the Phoenix area.

World headquarters of the Ace Hardware Corporation in Oak Brook, Illinois.

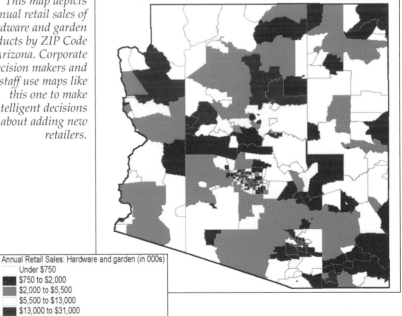

This map depicts annual retail sales of hardware and garden products by ZIP Code in Arizona. Corporate decision makers and field staff use maps like this one to make intelligent decisions about adding new retailers.

Annual Retail Sales: Hardware and garden (in 000s)
Under $750
$750 to $2,000
$2,000 to $5,500
$5,500 to $13,000
$13,000 to $31,000

Conducting the survey

The first step was to collect reliable data. Marketing research staff at Ace headquarters contracted with a Phoenix consultant to conduct interviews over a two-week period with shoppers leaving the Paradise Valley Ace store.

The survey (shown at right) asked people some questions about the shopping they'd just done and their impression of the store. To complete the survey, shoppers were asked for their home address (the few who didn't want to give it were excluded from the results). All the captured data would be of interest to the store's management, but it was the address component that made the information useful in ArcView GIS.

At the end of the second week, the store had over 200 completed survey forms, including addresses, to ship back to headquarters for tabulation, analysis, and mapping.

Paradise Valley Ace Survey

How long have you been shopping at this store for hardware and home improvement products?
- ❑ First time
- ❑ Less than 6 months
- ❑ 6 months to 1 year
- ❑ 1 year to 5 years
- ❑ More than 5 years

About how often do you shop at this store?
- ❑ More than once a week
- ❑ About once a week
- ❑ About once every two weeks
- ❑ About once a month
- ❑ Less than once a month/first time ever

What was the approximate total amount of your purchases today?
$_____

Are you shopping today for:
- ❑ Use at home
- ❑ Commercial
- ❑ Contractor

Overall, how would you rate this Ace Hardware store?
- ❑ Excellent
- ❑ Good
- ❑ Average
- ❑ Below average

Do you rent or own your living quarters?
- ❑ Rent
- ❑ Own

What is your home address and ZIP Code?
_____
_____

More than 200 survey forms like this one were filled out at the store and sent to corporate headquarters for analysis.

Mapping the customer database

Back at headquarters, an analyst entered the data (including the addresses) into an ArcView table. Each record in the table contained all the information for a single shopper. Using a Phoenix street map file from a commercial vendor, analysts next had ArcView GIS geocode, or plot on a map, the home addresses of all 200 respondents. The first map produced (shown on this page) displayed the geographic distribution of the surveyed customers.

Additional maps plotting data from each of the six questions were also created. While these maps were not used in the present study, they were part of the comprehensive package Ace delivered to the retailer.

To better understand the implications of the customer location data, analysts acquired ZIP Code and income files for the Phoenix area. When these were added to the customer map, some interesting facts came to light.

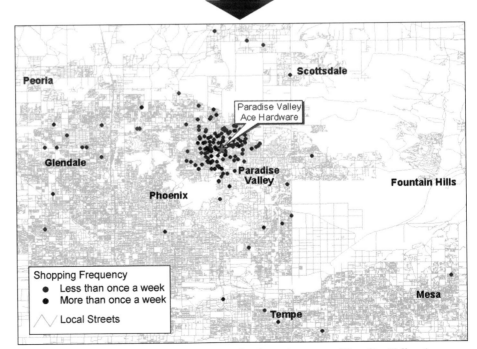

The survey results were entered in an ArcView table and geocoded onto a street map.

This map of the greater Phoenix area color-codes the main group of Paradise Valley Ace customers according to shopping frequency. The map shows, not surprisingly, that most shoppers live relatively close to the store.

The trade area revealed

The addition of ZIP Code boundaries to the map was of particular interest to the managers of Paradise Valley Ace Hardware, because it revealed that fully 85 percent of the surveyed customers came from one of three ZIP Codes (85032, 85254, or 85028)— a trade area considerably smaller than had been previously assumed.

Until this time, the store had been mailing a weekly advertising circular to about a dozen ZIP Codes covering a much wider area. The store's management immediately decided to restrict the mailing to just these three ZIP Codes. They reasoned that this would not adversely affect store traffic, since no other ZIP Codes (not even those currently hit with the direct mail piece) managed to deliver significant numbers of customers.

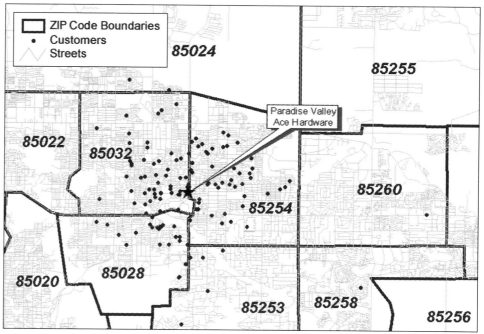

The cluster of points in ZIP Codes 85032, 85254, and 85028 reveals a trade area in which 85 percent of the surveyed customers live.

Mapping household income

In addition to the map of ZIP Code boundaries, the analysts also created a map of 1996 median household income, using census block group data from a vendor. A "block group" is a geographical designation used by the U.S. Census Bureau. It can be loosely thought of in terms of a neighborhood, and is the smallest area for which detailed demographic information is available.

Interestingly, this map showed a cluster of very high income ($100,000+) block groups located just a couple of miles south of the store. While the store managers already knew that this was a high-income area, they had no idea just how high until they saw the map.

However, the map also revealed that the store pulled very few customers from this high-income area. So, with the advertising dollars saved from scaling back the direct mail coverage, Paradise Valley Ace made plans for a special promotion.

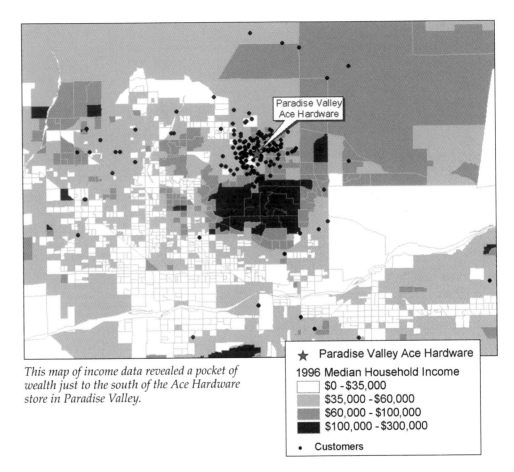

This map of income data revealed a pocket of wealth just to the south of the Ace Hardware store in Paradise Valley.

★ Paradise Valley Ace Hardware
1996 Median Household Income
- $0 - $35,000
- $35,000 - $60,000
- $60,000 - $100,000
- $100,000 - $300,000

• Customers

Acting on the information

Now that they knew about the nearby concentration of wealthy households, the store's managers needed to figure out how to reach these households. Their direct mail contractor could only target mailings by ZIP Code, so it wouldn't be possible to hit the high-income block groups exclusively.

The map at right gave them the clue they needed. It showed that the largest section of high-income block groups fell almost entirely within two adjacent ZIP Codes (85018 and 85253).

Reasoning that high-income households would be good candidates for home security systems, they put together a special mail piece offering an excellent deal on security systems and sent it to these two ZIP Codes.

The results were immediate: the store recouped the entire cost of the mailing within hours after opening on the first day of the promotion, and demand for security systems continued to be strong for several weeks afterward.

Based on this success, the store's management began planning future mailings to sell other items that would appeal to this income group.

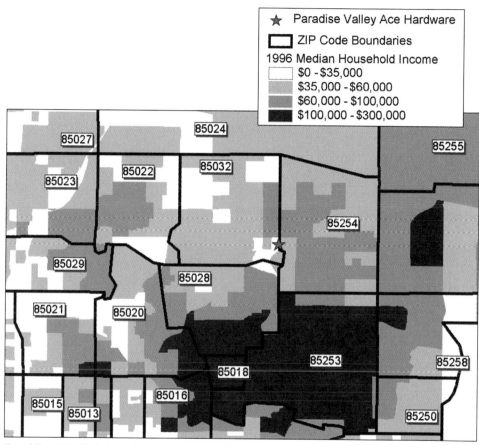

By adding ZIP Code boundaries to the map of high-income block groups, store managers saw that they could reach the bulk of the high-income households in their area by mailing to just two ZIP Codes.

Data

Retail sales figures provided by Equifax National Decision Systems, San Diego, California.

Dynamap/2000® street network data provided by Geographic Data Technology, Lyme, New Hampshire.

National Store List and Exit Survey for Paradise Valley Ace Hardware provided by Ace Hardware Corporation, Oak Brook, Illinois.

MarketPac-Express household income data provided by ESRI, Redlands, California.

Highways and ZIP Codes included with ArcView GIS.

Software

ArcView GIS for Windows®

Microsoft® Excel for Windows

Acknowledgments

Thanks to Bill Morreal, Amy Mortensen, and Dana Kevish of Ace Hardware Corporation.

Thanks, also, to Arthur Holm of Paradise Valley Ace Hardware.

Ace Hardware Corporation

Environmental Systems Research Institute, Inc.

Evaluating site suitability

The right location can mean the difference between success and failure. And selecting the ideal spot (often from among dozens of possibilities) can be a daunting task. The better you understand both your typical customer and the local demographics, the more intelligently you can choose or reject a given site. And if you operate a chain of stores, you want to know how a promising location will affect the revenues of your existing stores in the same area.

In this chapter, you'll see how a national fitness gym franchisor uses ArcView GIS to manage its contractual franchise agreements and to consider new franchise applications. You'll follow the process they used to evaluate a proposed new location and to measure how the new site would affect existing gyms.

Franchising at Gold's Gym

Gold's Gym Franchising, Inc. (Venice, California), is the world's largest gym chain, with over 500 locations worldwide.

The original Gold's Gym location, steps away from Venice's "Muscle Beach," quickly became a bodybuilding mecca. In 1975, Gold's was made famous by the movie "Pumping Iron" (the same film that launched Arnold Schwarzenegger's acting career).

Today there are Gold's Gyms in twenty-six countries. A line of licensed apparel products has helped make the Gold's Gym logo one of the most recognized in the world.

But merchandising success notwithstanding, the gym chain is still the company's crown jewel, so the business of licensing new franchises is taken very seriously.

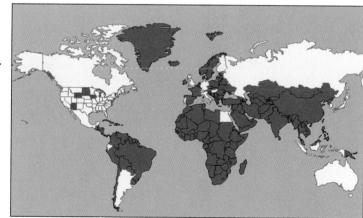

The world's most successful and well-known gym chain, Gold's Gym has locations in forty-three of the United States and in twenty-five other nations (highlighted in yellow) around the world.

Managing contractual agreements

Long Island, New York, is home to twelve Gold's Gym franchises. Each of these franchises has a "protected territory" in which Gold's Gym Franchising has contractually agreed not to allow another facility to be built. (The size and shape of a gym's protected territory varies according to the terms of the original contract, some of which date back as many as seventeen years.) Corporate staff in Venice maintain a digital map library of the U.S. market that shows the exact location of each franchise and the boundary of its protected territory.

When the corporate franchising manager received an application for a new gym on Long Island, his first task was to see where the proposed gym would be sited. Only if the site did *not* lie in a protected territory would the company even consider approving the new franchise. As shown in the map to the right, the proposed site was located in an unprotected area, albeit a small one.

With the contractual hurdle cleared, Gold's management could move on to a market analysis.

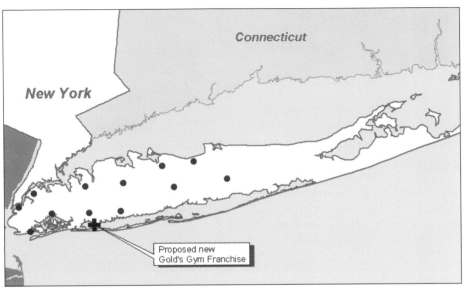

Red points mark each of the twelve existing Gold's locations on Long Island; the blue cross shows the location of the proposed franchise.

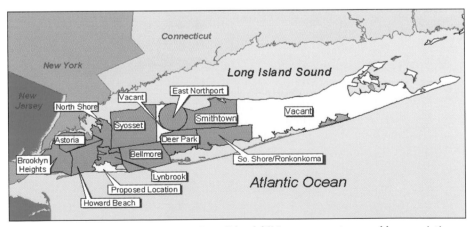

The proposed location in southwestern Long Island fell in an area not covered by an existing territory.

Environmental Systems Research Institute, Inc.

Working with competitive trade regions

Competitive trade regions are areas that segment the entire market on the basis of proximity to a given Gold's gym. In other words, a gym's competitive trade region encompasses all potential customers for whom that gym is the closest Gold's location. A competitive trade region is thus distinct from a protected territory (although the two areas are to some extent congruent).

In order to gauge how the new gym might affect the existing Gold's franchises on Long Island, analysts at the company's headquarters created a pair of maps representing the competitive trade regions: one showing the current situation and one showing what would change with the addition of the new gym.

These maps would be used to create before-and-after demographic profiles for each gym's competitive trade region.

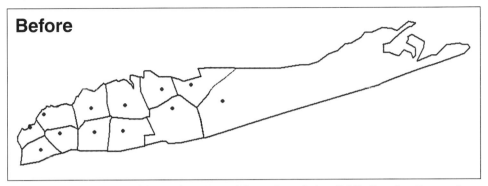

This map shows the competitive trade regions of the twelve existing Gold's Gym locations on Long Island.

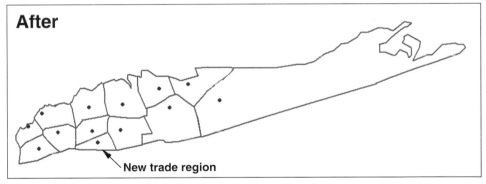

This map shows the impact of a thirteenth gym on the trade regions.

Selecting the demographic data

Gold's Gym has historically (and with great success) targeted the 17-to-39-year age group as its primary customers, with an emphasis on higher income earners.

Gold's keeps its demographic analysis simple and to the point by focusing on four variables: the total number of people in an area, people aged 17 to 39, people with health club memberships, and personal income. This data, broken down to the census block group level, is readily available commercially.

The analysts loaded a census block group map file of Long Island into ArcView GIS and linked it to a database table containing the relevant demographic information.

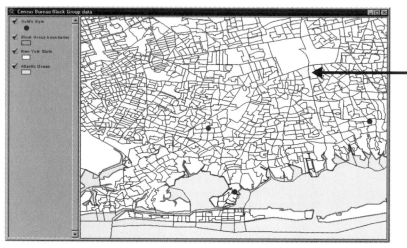

Shape	Block Group	Health club members	1996 Population	Age 17 to 39
Polygon	360594092.00:3	27	1057	397
Polygon	360594046.00:2	55	1583	509
Polygon	360594095.00:1	14	538	188
Polygon	360594073.02:1	38	1568	595
Polygon	360595205.02:4	30	891	271
Polygon	360594044.00:4	24	684	239
Polygon	360594069.00:1	16	1181	439
Polygon	360594069.00:4	15	1196	507
Polygon	360594094.00:1	20	755	250
Polygon	360594063.00:4	41	1143	291
Polygon	360594091.00:4	29	1015	391

In densely populated urban areas, block groups may contain anywhere from 500 to 2,000 people. Block group number 360594073.02:1, for example, was home to 1,568 people in 1996, over a third of whom were between the ages of 17 and 39.

Block group data is widely used for demographic analysis. Block groups are the smallest units for which the U.S. Census Bureau reports detailed statistics.

Measuring cannibalization

By superimposing (or *overlaying*) the competitive trade regions on the block groups, Gold's analysts next created two maps measuring how much of the market would be cannibalized by the new location. ("Cannibalization" refers to the phenomenon of a business stealing its own customers.) The simplifying, but reasonably accurate, assumption used in the analysis was that a customer will work out at the gym closest to him.

The upper map shows the demographics of the existing competitive trade regions. The lower map shows that a new location would cannibalize about 114,000 people from the Lynbrook and Bellmore gyms. Of the two, Lynbrook would be the harder hit, losing about 18 percent of its total market population.

Before making a final decision, Gold's management wanted to compare the demographics of the new location with the rest of the Gold's Gym franchises on Long Island.

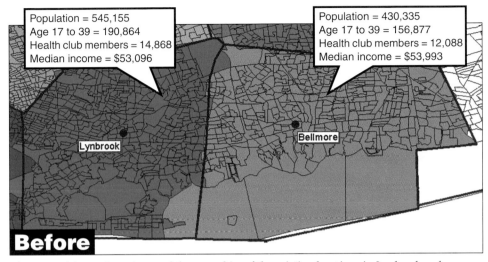

The competitive trade regions and demographics of the existing locations in Lynbrook and Bellmore.

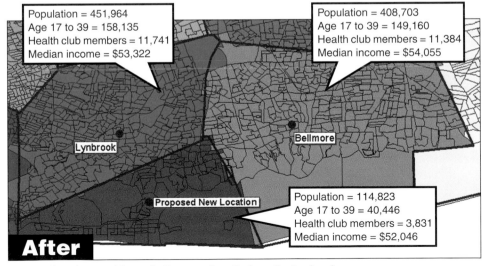

The new location would cannibalize most heavily from the Lynbrook gym.

Overall market area comparisons

The statistics for all the competitive trade regions on Long Island were computed using ArcView GIS and loaded into a single table (shown at right) for comparison. The proposed site, if opened, would rank fairly high in terms of median household income and the percentage of people in the target age group. But in terms of sheer numerical strength, the site was significantly weaker than most of the other locations on Long Island. In fact, the new site would rank dead last in terms of total population.

The result was that the franchising manager could make a well-grounded decision *not* to approve the new franchise. While the existing locations could probably survive the cannibalization, the new site simply did not have a large enough population to support it. The only gym with a smaller base of health club members in its trade region was the one in Smithtown, a rural area with many fewer competitors than southwestern Long Island.

Thanks to a sound methodology and GIS, the decision was simple and straightforward.

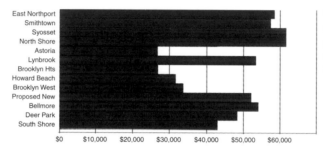

Name	Population	Age 17-39	Median income	Health club members	% age 17-39
East Northport	169771	59980	58405	5474	0.35
Smithtown	119814	46430	57424	3538	0.39
Syosset	240249	83228	61609	7417	0.35
North Shore	260760	83717	61633	8980	0.32
Astoria	927978	370168	26687	24851	0.40
Lynbrook	451964	158135	53322	11741	0.35
Brooklyn Heights	1140654	450848	26878	29077	0.40
Howard Beach	804690	300936	31530	18385	0.37
Brooklyn West	646540	217112	33617	18404	0.34
Proposed New	114823	40446	52046	3831	0.35
Bellmore	408703	149160	54055	11384	0.36
Deer Park	394997	152437	48269	9546	0.39
South Shore	374696	143302	42889	10193	0.38

Demographic data on the proposed location and the existing locations is stored in a table.

The corporate franchise manager was presented with a series of bar charts comparing each of the relevant demographic variables (in this case, household income).

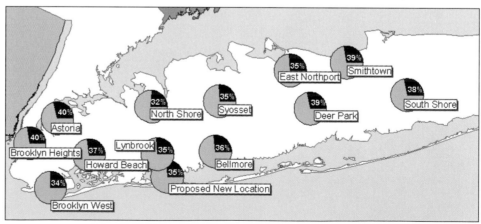

This pie chart map displays the 17-to-39 age group as a percentage of the total population in each trade region.

Data

FIRST ST.™ desktop mapping software block group boundaries for New York provided by Wessex, Winnetka, Illinois.

Current-year demographics provided by Equifax National Decision Systems, San Diego, California.

Software

ArcView GIS for Windows

Acknowledgments

Thanks to Paul Grymkowski of Gold's Gym Franchising, Inc.

Increasing newspaper readership

Daily newspapers—once the primary source of most people's information—today face intense competition from a variety of other media. As newspaper readership declines nationally, publishers must work harder to attract and retain subscribers. While some traditional print publishers have successfully introduced electronic editions of their news products, the printed paper, delivered to the doorstep, is still the main source of revenue for most metropolitan daily newspapers. So finding new readers is essential to keeping the business profitable.

In this chapter, you'll see how one publisher created digital boundary maps of its delivery routes with ArcView GIS, then used these maps to analyze readership patterns and successfully target new customers.

The hunt for new subscribers

The Press-Enterprise Co. (Riverside, California) has put out a newspaper every day since 1885. Serving all of Riverside County, California, the paper covers a huge market that includes both urban and rural sectors. With a circulation of over 160,000, *The Press-Enterprise* has the largest readership among several competing dailies in the area.

In recent years, however, circulation hasn't quite kept pace with population growth, and this has caused the company some concern. Management called on its marketing research staff to contribute to the discussions about

the circulation issue. They decided to use GIS to map their customer database and analyze the demographics of their market. The goal was to find areas that were rich in potential new subscribers.

The Press-Enterprise *used ArcView GIS to locate concentrations of likely subscribers in the fast-growing Riverside County, California, daily newspaper market.*

Mapping the carrier routes

The Press-Enterprise Circulation Department manages deliveries according to a system of numbered carrier routes. Carrier routes are also the basic unit the department uses to report and study circulation. Thus, the first step in the project was to create a map of carrier routes.

Every address in the paper's entire market area, whether it belongs to a subscriber or not, is kept in a database and assigned to a particular carrier route. Working from this database of deliverable addresses, the market analysts used ArcView GIS to convert each address into a point on a street map, a process called *geocoding*. Because every address record in the database can be identified by its carrier route, the points could be color-coded to create the map at the bottom.

This map, although impressive, was just an intermediate product: it didn't yet show the carrier routes as areas with distinct boundaries.

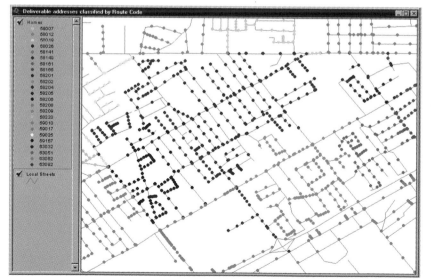

ArcView GIS automatically converts the paper's database of deliverable addresses into points on a commercially available digital street map. The database is dynamically linked to the map display, which means that any information in the database can be visually represented.

The Route Code field in the database was used to classify the addresses by color on the basis of the carrier route they belonged to. A set of points of the same color thus defined the geographic area of a carrier route.

The GIS staff then used an add-on product, called ArcView Spatial Analyst, to draw a *continuous-surface* map, in which each set of points was covered by a different polygon. The outlines of the polygons, defining the boundaries of the carrier routes, were extracted and saved as a new map file in ArcView GIS.

Now the analysts had what they wanted—a map that would be useful for displaying and studying subscription information.

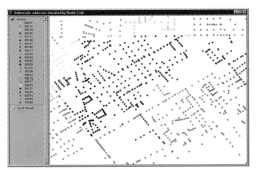

Every deliverable address is represented as a colored point. Points of the same color belong to the same carrier route.

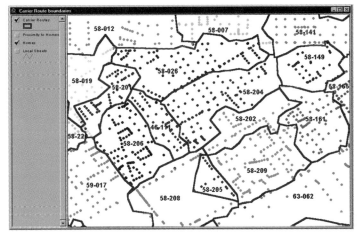

The outlines of the polygons are the boundaries of the carrier routes.

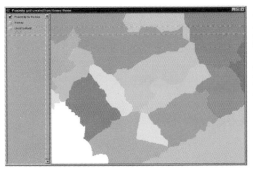

ArcView Spatial Analyst draws a polygon over each uniquely colored set of points. The polygons form a continuous surface covering the entire market.

Analyzing subscriber data

The next step was to link the map of carrier route boundaries to the company's table of circulation data—the number of homes in the area, the number of subscribers, and the ratio of subscribers to homes. The map on this page displays the carrier routes in a section of Riverside. It shows areas in white and blue where the subscription rate was less than 45 percent.

But this was still only half the story. To see which routes offered the most potential for gain, the analysts needed to see how many people in each route matched the profile of the typical *Press-Enterprise* reader.

To find this out, they added some demographic data to the model.

Route Code	Homes	Subscriptions	% Reach
58-007	282	128	0.45
58-141	334	151	0.45
58-012	338	156	0.46
58-149	306	123	0.40
58-026	431	195	0.45
58-019	184	108	0.59
58-201	191	117	0.61
58-165	331	149	0.45
58-204	309	188	0.61
58-202	397	112	0.28
58-161	280	153	0.55
58-220	274	181	0.66
58-206	217	132	0.61
58-205	274	112	0.41
58-209	249	154	0.62

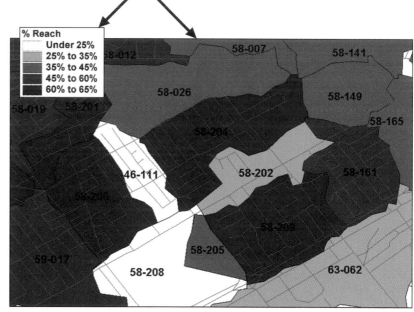

% Reach
- Under 25%
- 25% to 35%
- 35% to 45%
- 45% to 60%
- 60% to 65%

This map divides the carrier routes into five classes according to the percentage of subscribers they contain. The data can be broken into more or fewer classes as desired; specific value ranges for each class can also be set.

Incorporating demographic data

The paper's latest market study showed that most people who read *The Press-Enterprise* fall into one or more of four demographic categories: people aged 55 to 70, people living in households with annual incomes above $50,000, home owners, and college graduates. Demographic data on these variables for Riverside County was purchased for the project. The only problem was that the data was broken down by census block groups, and the analysts needed to see it broken down by carrier route.

With the help of ArcView Spatial Analyst, the map of carrier routes was overlaid on a map of census block groups covering the same area. The demographic data for the block groups was mathematically reapportioned among the carrier routes according to the complex ways in which they overlapped (bottom graphic).

At this point, the analysts had everything they needed: a map of carrier routes that was linked both to actual subscription data and to data defining the typical customer. They were now ready to evaluate each route by its potential for increased sales.

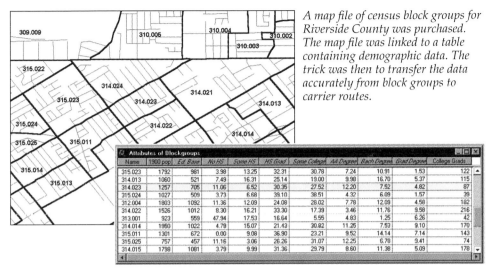

A map file of census block groups for Riverside County was purchased. The map file was linked to a table containing demographic data. The trick was then to transfer the data accurately from block groups to carrier routes.

Attributes of Blockgroups

Name	1900 pop	Ed Base	No HS	Some HS	HS Grad	Some College	AA Degree	Bach Degree	Grad Degree	College Grads
315.023	1792	981	3.98	13.25	32.31	30.78	7.24	10.91	1.53	122
314.013	1060	521	7.49	16.31	25.14	19.00	9.98	16.70	5.37	115
314.023	1257	705	11.06	6.52	30.35	27.52	12.20	7.52	4.82	87
315.024	1027	509	3.73	6.68	39.10	38.51	4.32	6.09	1.57	39
312.004	1803	1092	11.36	12.09	24.08	28.02	7.78	12.09	4.58	182
314.022	1526	1012	8.30	16.21	33.30	17.39	3.46	11.76	9.58	216
313.001	923	559	47.94	17.53	16.64	5.55	4.83	1.25	6.26	42
314.014	1950	1022	4.79	15.07	21.43	30.82	11.25	7.53	9.10	170
315.011	1301	672	0.00	9.08	36.90	23.21	9.52	14.14	7.14	143
315.025	757	457	11.16	3.06	26.26	31.07	12.25	6.78	3.41	74
314.015	1798	1081	3.79	9.99	31.36	29.79	8.60	11.38	5.09	178

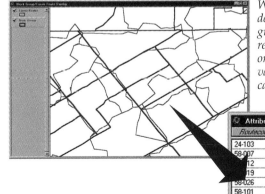

With ArcView Spatial Analyst, the demographic values for the census block groups (shown in blue) were proportionally reassigned to the carrier routes (shown in red) on the basis of shared geography. The new values were stored in a table linked to the carrier route map file.

Attributes of Carrier Routes

Routecode	$50,000 plus	Owner Occupied	College Grads	Age 55 plus
24-103	112	146	67	71
58-007	206	405	104	310
12	227	375	110	252
19	178	306	96	218
58-026	208	310	60	257
58-101	151	323	57	190
58-102	13	24	7	19
58-109	193	327	86	179
58-121	323	528	226	495
58-126	216	345	188	302

Comparing actual to potential subscription

To fully depict the situation, three maps were needed: a map of actual subscribers, a map of subscriber profile, and a map combining the two to find where actual subscription was low, but potential was high. The maps on this page show the Riverside Metro zone of *The Press-Enterprise,* an area containing about 200 carrier routes. (The paper's other seven zones were mapped separately.)

The top map (like the map on page 32) uses data from the circulation database to shade the carrier routes according to the percentage of subscribers they contain. Bright red areas have the lowest subscription rates; light red areas have the highest.

To create the bottom map, the four demographic variables of interest were weighted equally and combined to form an index of overall subscription potential. The carrier routes shaded bright red had the best scores—in other words, they contained the highest percentages of typical subscribers, or people likely to read *The Press-Enterprise.*

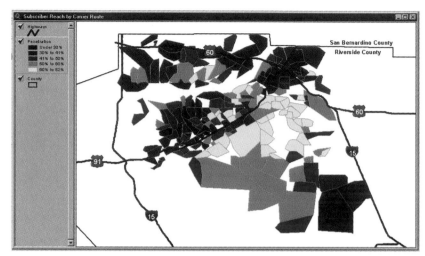

This map ranks the carrier routes by actual subscription levels, with dark red representing the areas of lowest penetration.

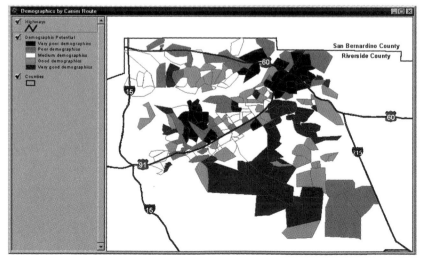

This map ranks the carrier routes by demographic potential. Red and light red areas contain a high percentage of people who typify the Press-Enterprise *subscriber.*

Environmental Systems Research Institute, Inc.

The analysts then combined the maps of actual subscribers and subscriber profile to produce a map ranking the carrier routes by their potential for circulation gain. Bright red areas have the best combination of good demographics and low circulation, pale red areas are next best, and so on.

Accompanying the map is a table sorting the carrier routes according to the same formula. This is the actual table that management used to dispatch door-to-door sales crews.

Verifying the results in the field

The first crews sent into the top-ranked areas came back with nearly twice the new subscriptions of the previous year's crews. Based on the success of the Riverside Metro project, the analysis was eventually rolled out to all of the paper's other seven circulation zones.

The experience of *The Press-Enterprise* is a clear-cut example of the impact that a well-designed GIS project can have on sales.

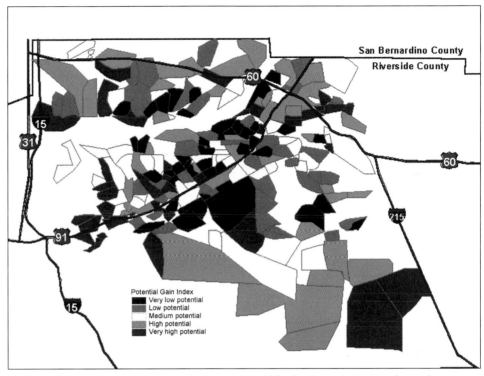

The final map indicates where sales crews should be sent. Carrier routes shown in red contain the highest concentrations of likely readers who are not currently subscribing to The Press-Enterprise.

Routecode	Potential Gain Index	Routepen	Totdx
59-440	207	0.34	150
C-131	206	0.22	107
59-493	200	0.34	147
C-072	196	0.24	105
64-038	195	0.28	104
C-071	195	0.24	103
58-208	194	0.21	86
64-232	191	0.21	85
64-218	189	0.14	73
59-240	189	0.40	147
59-267	185	0.31	108
59-292	179	0.27	86
67-100	176	0.20	69
58-231	176	0.17	66
70-014	175	0.28	89
69-602	174	0.37	131
70-090	173	0.30	101
70-043	172	0.31	107
70-056	167	0.41	145
59-036	166	0.19	60

Data

Dynamap/2000 street network data provided by Geographic Data Technology, Lyme, New Hampshire.

PopFacts on CD demographic variables by block group provided by Equifax National Decision Systems, San Diego, California.

Software

ArcView GIS for Windows

ArcView Spatial Analyst for Windows

Acknowledgments

Thanks to Michael Schuerman and Robert Perona of The Press-Enterprise Company.

THE PRESS-ENTERPRISE

Environmental Systems Research Institute, Inc.

Finding new banking opportunities

Perhaps no industries in the world are as complex, or change as quickly, as banking and financial services. The most successful companies in this field have entire departments dedicated to making sense of the constant stream of market information. If you think getting through *The Wall Street Journal* every morning is a chore, try being a research analyst at a global bank and you'll see what data overload is really like. Leading financial institutions are increasingly discovering the unique ability of GIS to help them visualize market situations, analyze data, and build realistic models that predict how changes in strategy might affect their business.

In this chapter, you'll see how a large bank used ArcView GIS to study one of its branch locations in an urban micromarket, and how it pinpointed a significant opportunity by focusing on the market's daytime population.

GIS in banking

With over $300 billion in assets, The Chase Manhattan Bank (New York, New York) is the largest bank in the United States. In addition to being one of the nation's leaders in consumer finance (credit cards, mortgage banking, auto and student loans), Chase is also the New York City leader in consumer banking, where deposit and investment products are sold through branch locations in urban and suburban markets.

To stay on top, Chase conducts regular reviews of its branch business, evaluating the performance and

potential of each location through its Distribution Planning department. During one such review, of a branch on Manhattan's East Side, Chase analysts used GIS to discover some interesting things about the branch's customer base—and to identify an unforeseen marketing opportunity.

Chase Manhattan Bank uses GIS to study all parts of its consumer business. An analysis of one section of New York City looked at both the daytime and nighttime populations, to better see the potential for deposits in the area.

Building the geographic model

The GIS component of a branch review involves defining a trade area around the branch, measuring the market potential within that trade area, and identifying the nearby competitors. (A trade area is the area from which a business draws most of its customers.)

To begin the process, analysts at Chase made an ArcView map of the vicinity that included census tract boundaries, as well as physical geography, like streets and natural landmarks.

The census tracts would be used as the building blocks from which to construct the trade area. Later, they would serve as a framework for adding data to the market potential analysis.

Next, the locations of competitors were added to the map, followed by symbols representing Chase's own branches—including, of course, the branch under review.

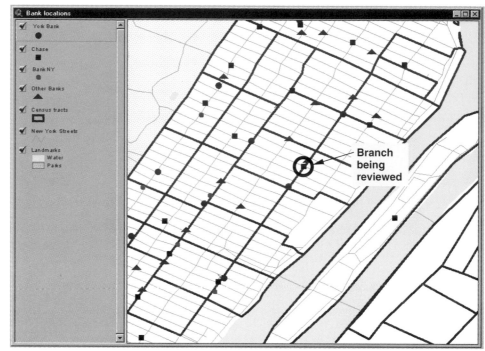

Putting the required geographic data into ArcView GIS was the first step in the market analysis of a Chase branch in New York City.

Determining the trade area

Now the analysts were ready to define the branch's trade area. This is commonly done by drawing a circle that includes most of the known customer addresses around the location in question. Chase, however, was able to use a more sophisticated method, relying on a proprietary database that told them where their customers conducted transactions and held accounts.

In this case, 64 percent of the branch's customers lived in one of the seven census tracts shown in green. But the other 36 percent were drawn from the local work force—they came into the trade area each day and left at night. This told the analysts that a sizeable fraction of their customers banked where they worked rather than where they lived—in other words, that the area's daytime population constituted a significant market.

With the trade area thus determined, and insight gained as to the nature of the customer base, it was time to add demographic and financial data to the analysis.

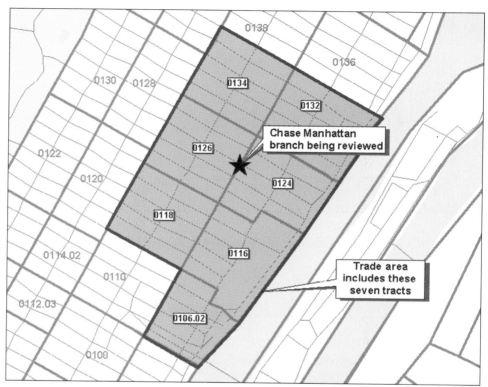

More than a third of the customers of the Chase branch lived outside the trade area and came from the daytime population. (Note that the bank locations aren't shown on this map. In ArcView GIS, individual data sets can be displayed, or not, according to the needs of the moment.)

Measuring market potential

The analysts' next step was to look at data on the "nighttime," or resident, population of the trade area. It showed that there were more than 36,000 households controlling about $1.5 billion in potential deposits, and that tract 0126 was easily the best of the seven, with over $400 million in

potential deposits. The Chase branch, situated as it was on the edge of this tract, was well-positioned to serve the 8,000 households located there.

When the analysts then turned their attention to the daytime population, they found out something interesting.

One tract (0116) swelled with over 14,000 workers every day because it contained two medical centers. Moreover, these 14,000 workers (together with their households) controlled over half a billion dollars in potential deposits.

Deposit Product Demand ("Nighttime" resident population)

Shape	Tract	Households	Deposit Product Demand ($ millions)
Polygon	0134.00	6547	257.5
Polygon	0132.00	5928	241.9
Polygon	0126.00	8087	418.7
Polygon	0124.00	6133	219.4
Polygon	0118.00	5280	264.0
Polygon	0116.00	2449	67.5
Polygon	0106.02	2052	84.9

This table shows the number of households living in each census tract of the trade area, along with their deposit product demand (that is, the amount of money they have available for deposit).

Area contains a total of:

- 36,500 households accounting for $1.5 billion in potential deposits
- 36,000 daytime workers accounting for $1.4 billion in potential deposits

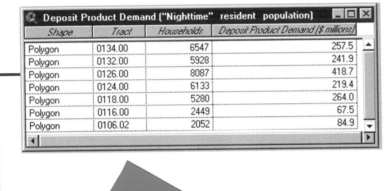

Deposit Product Demand ("Daytime" worker population)

Shape	Tract	Daytime workers	Deposit Product Demand ($ millions)
Polygon	0134.00	3849	126.6
Polygon	0132.00	2923	98.5
Polygon	0126.00	3892	177.6
Polygon	0124.00	3229	233.1
Polygon	0118.00	4592	158.3
Polygon	0116.00	14912	527.6
Polygon	0106.02	2475	70.6

This table shows the daytime population, or the number of people who work in each tract, and the deposits they control. Note the large number in tract 0116.

Comparing day and night populations

The analysts next created a pair of maps (one for nighttime, one for daytime) that classified the census tracts by their deposit potential and showed the locations of the hospitals in the area.

The two maps contrasted the difference in potential deposits controlled by the nighttime and daytime populations. They showed management that the influx of daytime workers into tract 0116 had an enormous impact on the situation. In fact, this impact was so great as to transform tract 0116 from the lowest ranking nighttime tract into far and away the highest ranking daytime tract.

It was therefore clear that the daytime population of tract 0116 (largely composed of the people who worked at the Ewing Memorial and New York Hospitals) represented a major marketing opportunity. The analysts now needed to reexamine the locations of their competitors to see how well the other banks were positioned to compete for this market.

This map shows the highest concentration of nighttime population potential deposits to be in tract 0126.

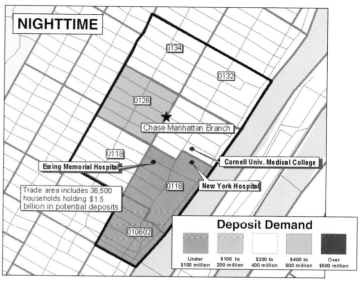

This map of daytime population, in contrast, shows the potential deposits to be highest in tract 0116.

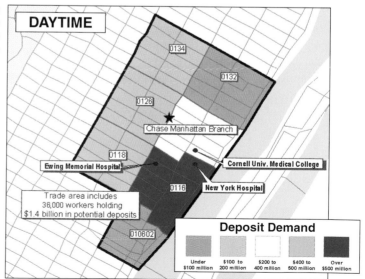

Seizing the daytime

After displaying and labeling their competitors' locations, the analysts zoomed in on census tract 0116. The map showed that one competitor (York Bank) had a branch on the corner of the tract—and was thus three blocks closer to the tract's work force. In an urban micromarket dominated by foot traffic, three blocks is a considerable advantage.

As a result of the analysis, Chase studied several different ways to capitalize on the opportunity. One possibility was to relocate the Chase branch to a site closer to the target tract. A recommendation was made to have the firm's real estate department look at price and availability of suitable locations in the area.

Another option was to develop a marketing plan that would strengthen Chase's relationships with the large medical institutions in the area. This plan might go so far as to offer the bank's services directly to employees at work.

Whatever the ultimate decision, GIS played a major role in bringing the situation to light. It was Chase's own customer database that established the importance of the daytime population to the branch's business. But it was ArcView GIS that pointed analysts to the huge concentration of hospital workers in the area, and that let them instantly compare their proximity to this market with that of their competitors.

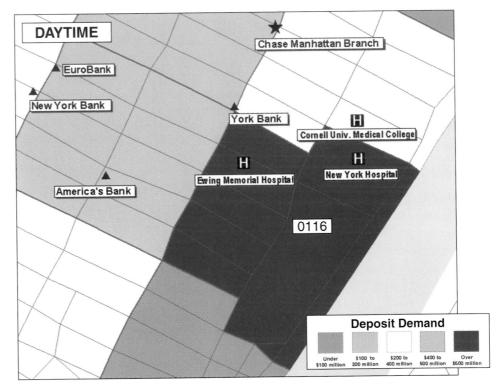

The high deposit demand represented by the two medical centers in tract 0116 was a significant opportunity for Chase Manhattan.

Data

FIRST ST. desktop mapping software local streets and census tracts data provided by Wessex, Winnetka, Illinois.

Software

ArcView GIS for Windows

Acknowledgments

Thanks to the Distribution Planning Group of Chase Manhattan Bank.

Realigning sales territories

There's no such thing as a product that sells itself. Companies live and die by their sales forces, which means that their account reps need to spend as much time with customers (and as little time on the road) as possible. This goal can be largely achieved through sales territories that make geographic sense: ones from which a salesperson can conveniently reach all her customers.

In this chapter, you'll see how a national manufacturer of printing inks used ArcView GIS and a custom software package to analyze and redraw its sales territories, thereby obtaining major gains in sales force productivity.

Improving sales force productivity

Ink Tech (Tampa, Florida) is a producer of specialized inks used in industrial printing processes. With branch offices located throughout the United States, the company sells its products directly to printers and sign makers.

In the greater Chicago area, four sales reps, working mainly out of their homes, serve approximately 1,900 accounts in northern Illinois and northwestern Indiana.

In the past, salespeople had often been assigned to accounts on the basis of perceived application expertise, or who "needed" accounts. As a result, some accounts were so far away that the reps spent more time driving to and from their appointments than they spent with clients. Even worse, the hours they were putting in on the road left them little or no time to prospect for new accounts. Ink Tech decided to seek the advice of a consultant.

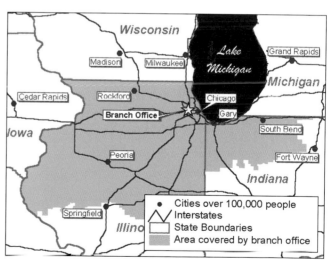

Management brought in productivity specialists to evaluate Ink Tech's sales territories. The area shown here is the territory covered by the branch office.

Defining the problem

The consulting firm (Wilkening & Company, Park Ridge, Illinois) began the analysis by looking at a customer database of the accounts served by the branch office.

The database listed the name and location of each account, how much it had bought in the previous year, and which salesperson calls upon the account.

The first thing the consultants wanted to see was exactly where the accounts were and to whom they belonged. They loaded the customer database into ArcView GIS and used each account's ZIP Code information to represent it as a point on a map (a process known as *geocoding*). Each point was then color-coded according to the sales rep who handled the account.

What the map showed was that there were really no "territories" at all; instead, each of the reps roamed widely over the two-state market.

Plotting the customers on a map also revealed that about 130 accounts fell outside the branch office's market area. These accounts were later reassigned to other company branches or to independent distributors.

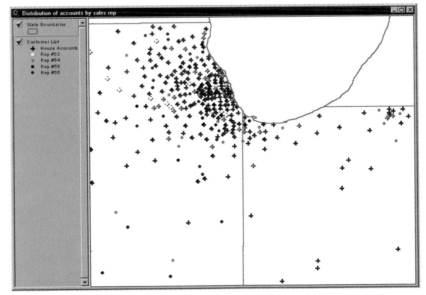

Customer list					
Customer	City	State	Zip	Sales Rep#	Previous year's sales
COLOR WEAR	SKOKIE	IL	60076	56	2451.00
EMCO ENTERPRISES	MT.PROSPECT	IL	60056	54	2906.00
JJ FEELINGS	HIGHWOOD	IL	60040	5	0.00
GANDRUD PRESS	EVANSTON	IL	60202	54	8196.00
DESIGN PLACE	CHICAGO	IL	60641	53	389.00
DESIGN SPORTSWEAR	ARLINGTON HTS	IL	60004	55	1343.00
A-8 INCORPORATED	CHICAGO	IL	60614	55	1500.00
NUSAFE INDUSTRIES	MUNDELEIN	IL	60060	54	1970.00
UPPERDECK	GLENVIEW	IL	60025	54	43048.00
ILLINOIS DECAL & MFG CO	CHICAGO	IL	60639	54	3117.00
S I HENRICKSEN	WAUKEGAN	IL	60085	54	32770.00
ORMSBY DISPLAY	CHICAGO	IL	60657	54	12162.00
HANSEN BINDERY	WAUKEGAN	IL	60087	54	4935.00

The customer database contains the code number of the rep assigned to each account. A "5" in the Sales Rep# field means that the account is unassigned; unassigned accounts are handled either by an in-house sales group or by the branch manager.

There's no pattern to the way accounts are distributed among the sales reps. By restructuring territories, the company can cut down on the amount of time each rep spends on the road.

Quantifying the overlap

Because the customer database contained both the ZIP Code and sales rep information for each account, analysts could use ArcView GIS to find the number of reps making calls in each ZIP Code. Put on a map, this data showed plainly how much the accounts near metro Chicago overlapped, something that had been difficult to see on the previous map. In the most extreme cases (shown in red), all four sales reps had active accounts in the same ZIP Code.

The consultants' goal was to design new territories that made geographic sense, but since the accounts weren't spread evenly throughout the market, simply creating four new jurisdictions of equal size wouldn't work. Nor would dividing the number of accounts by four and then drawing geographic boundaries around them. (Some of the accounts were large and needed lots of attention, while others

were small and needed little.) So in addition to organizing the new territories by geography, the consultants

had to structure them in such a way that the reps had relatively balanced workloads.

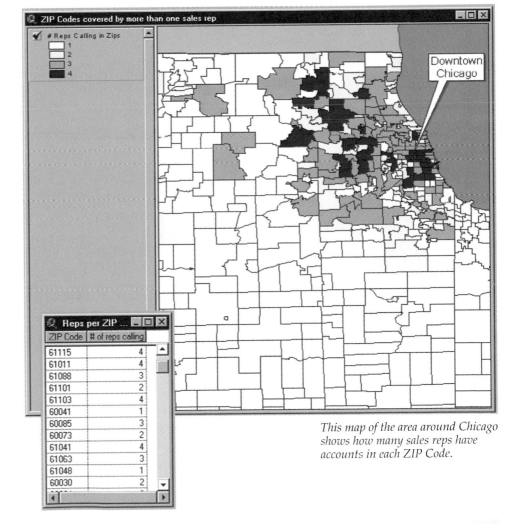

This map of the area around Chicago shows how many sales reps have accounts in each ZIP Code.

Establishing account size and service goals

Ink Tech sales reps were asked to divide their accounts into four classes, A through D, according to how much business they expected the accounts to generate in the coming year. Their evaluations were based on data from the customer database as well as personal knowledge of the accounts.

Planning guidelines				
Potential	Class	Annual # of visits	Length of avg visit	Annual contact required
$50,000 plus	A	12	1.5	18.0
$10,000 to $49,999	B	9	1.0	9.0
$3,000 to $9,000	C	4	0.5	2.0
Under $3,000	D	1	0.5	0.5

The planning guidelines table created four classes of accounts based on anticipated sales. Goals were set for the number of visits and time per visit the accounts in each class should receive.

The consultants then met with the branch manager and the sales reps to determine how much contact time each account should receive, according to its class. (It was decided, for example, that Class "A" accounts should be called on twelve times a year, for a total of eighteen hours.) These figures, understood to be guidelines, not exact formulas, were then entered into a "planning guidelines" table.

Customer list						
Customer	City	State	Zip	Sales Rep#	Previous year's sale	Class
COLOR WEAR	SKOKIE	IL	60076	56	2451.00	D
EMCO ENTERPRISES	MT.PROSPECT	IL	60056	54	2906.00	D
JJ FEELINGS	HIGHWOOD	IL	60040	5	0.00	D
GANDRUD PRESS	EVANSTON	IL	60202	54	8196.00	C
DESIGN PLACE	CHICAGO	IL	60641	53	389.00	D
DESIGN SPORTSWEAR	ARLINGTON HTS	IL	60004	55	1343.00	D
A-8 INCORPORATED	CHICAGO	IL	60614	55	1500.00	D
NUSAFE INDUSTRIES	MUNDELEIN	IL	60060	54	1970.00	D

A new field was added to the customer table to store each account's class rating. This table was then merged with the planning guidelines table so that each account's record also showed the planning guidelines that applied to it.

Next, a new field containing each account's rating (A through D) was added to the customer database. The planning guidelines table was then merged with the customer table; from this merged database the consultants were able to generate an "account summary" table. This table subtotaled each rep's current accounts by class, and calculated the total contact time needed to service all accounts. This information would be used to balance the workloads.

Account summary						
Rep	"A" Accounts	"B" Accounts	"C" Accounts	"D" Accounts	All accounts	Total contact time
Rep 5	5	11	18	491	525	470
Rep 53	14	41	49	216	320	827
Rep 54	8	26	43	100	177	514
Rep 55	7	27	50	231	315	584
Rep 56	0	15	36	489	540	451

From the merged table (not shown), ArcView GIS generated this table that breaks down each rep's existing accounts by class. The table also shows the number of hours the reps would have to work to service their accounts according to the planning guidelines.

Environmental Systems Research Institute, Inc.

Balancing the workloads

The consultants put the account summary information and other data into a proprietary Wilkening & Company software package called *Sales Atlas*. This program simulates travel and sales call time. It runs through each salesperson's daily workload for a year, showing how much time it should take each rep to do her job. If a rep uses one day per workweek for sales meetings, training, correspondence, and other administrative duties, 200 workdays are available to conduct field calls and new account prospecting.

The analysis showed that the existing workloads were not balanced. One rep (#53) had over 200 field days of work, while the others had between 152 and 164 days. This meant that rep #53 had no time to prospect for new customers, while the other reps had about 40 days of prospecting time available each year.

It was also discovered that each of the reps spent too much time traveling and not enough meeting with clients. (This was not surprising in light of how they crisscrossed the entire market.)

The consultants now had the information they needed to help the company design new sales territories.

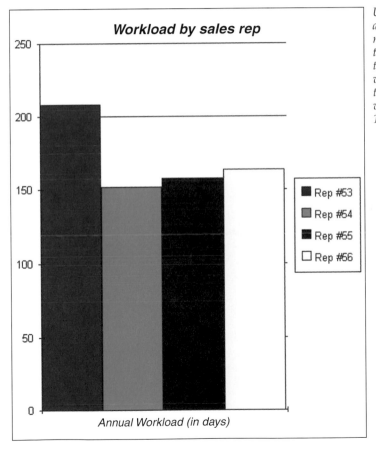

Under the existing assignments, rep #53 needed to work more than 200 days a year to meet expectations, while the remaining three reps needed to work between 152 and 164 days a year.

Creating the new territories

The Wilkening & Company consultants had two main objectives for the new territories. One was to make sure that the workloads were distributed as evenly as possible. The other was to cut down the time the reps spent on the road. This would give them more time to call on clients and prospect for new customers. It would also enable them to take over the unassigned accounts.

Using ArcView GIS, the consultants built test territories around each rep's home by forming clusters of adjoining ZIP Codes. The accounts (including those that had previously been unassigned) were allocated to the reps on the basis of proximity to their homes. The new assignments were then run through the *Sales Atlas* simulator to see if the workloads were balanced. The ZIP Code clusters were then modified, and the process repeated, until the workload for each rep was approximately the same.

Sometimes the existing rapport between a salesperson and a client was important enough to override the newly drawn sales territories. In these cases, the accounts remained in the hands of their original reps. Ink Tech didn't want improved efficiency to come at the expense of valuable business relationships.

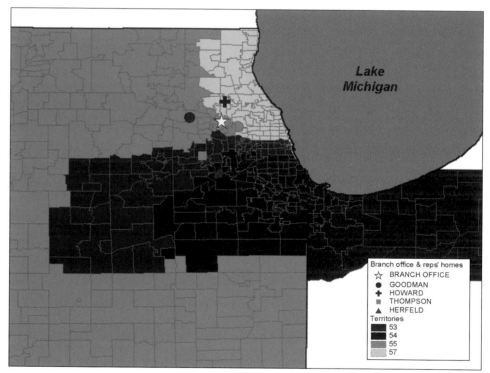

Using ArcView GIS to select clusters of adjacent ZIP Codes, the consultants experimented with different designs. The resulting territories, shown here, provided the best combination of low travel time and evenly distributed workload.

The result

Implementing the new sales territory design saved Ink Tech money right away in reduced travel expenses.

The reps cut their collective travel time by over 400 hours in the first year. This savings allowed them to devote greater attention to their existing accounts (in accordance with the planning guidelines) and to spend more time prospecting for new customers. In addition, they were able to pick up hundreds of unassigned accounts.

All Ink Tech sales planning is now conducted in the context of geography.

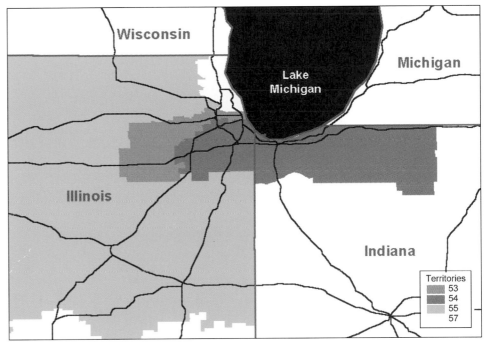

The new territories differ considerably in size, but the workloads are balanced. And by calling on accounts that are close to where they live, rather than traversing the entire market area, the reps are able to spend more time with more customers.

Data

FIRST ST. desktop mapping software streets and highways, states, and county boundaries data provided by Wessex, Winnetka, Illinois.

Five-digit ZIP Code boundaries data from *Data and Maps* CD–ROM (included with ArcView GIS), ESRI.

Software

ArcView GIS for Windows

Sales Atlas for Windows provided by Wilkening & Company, Park Ridge, Illinois.

Acknowledgments

Ink Tech is a fictitious company name. The analysis was actually conducted as described by the consultant for a client who requested anonymity.

Thanks to Bob Wilkening of Wilkening & Company.

Wilkening & Company

CHAPTER 7

Evaluating health care resources

As the American population grows and grays, health care organizations have to come up with new ways to practice good medicine while staying financially sound. One popular model is managed care, where doctors, hospitals, and other providers join cooperative, often centralized, groups to deliver health services more efficiently. GIS technology is becoming an important tool in managed care because of its ability to analyze the relationships between demand (patients) and resources (providers) according to location.

In this chapter, you'll see how a large hospital in the Pacific Northwest used ArcView GIS to evaluate how well its facilities were situated with respect to a specific group of patients, and how ArcView helped identify the best location for a new facility to be built in the next five years.

GIS in health care

St. Peter Hospital (Olympia, Washington) is the nucleus of a medical service complex that includes more than 200 physician offices, a major HMO, a large multispecialty clinic, a radiation therapy facility, nursing homes, and a variety of allied businesses. Part of the Sisters of Providence health care system, St. Peter serves a five-county area that is home to nearly half a million people.

Despite its nonprofit status, St. Peter is subject to the same market pressures faced by its privately owned competitors. So, as part of its efforts to adapt to the changing health care environment, St. Peter established a Decision Support group to conduct research and present recommendations to hospital management. Increasingly, this group has come to rely on GIS as a tool for analyzing the geographic relationships between patients and facilities.

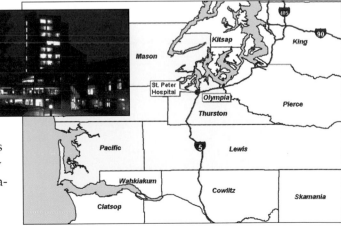

St. Peter Hospital in Olympia, Washington, operates a number of facilities throughout a five-county service area in the southern part of the state.

Analyzing the demand for dialysis treatment

Recently, Decision Support was asked to evaluate how well the hospital's two dialysis units were serving patients with end-stage renal failure (kidney disease). People with this condition need regular hemodialysis treatment, which essentially does the kidneys' work of cleaning the blood of toxins. Without a transplant, patients must have regular treatment at a licensed dialysis center in order to survive.

Because St. Peter currently delivers 95 percent of all dialysis treatment to patients living in the five-county area, management wanted a detailed analysis of demand, both current and long-term.

To carry out the project, the Decision Support group used ArcView GIS to map current demand and see if it was being adequately met; they then went on to find the areas where expected population growth would create the most demand for future dialysis units.

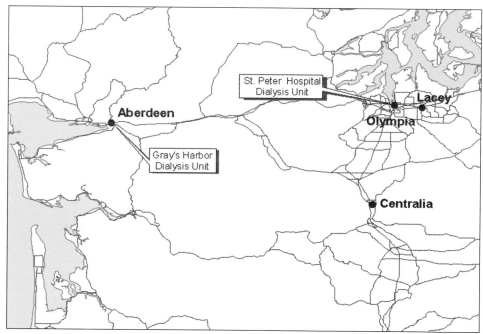

St. Peter operates two hemodialysis units in the greater Olympia area: one at its hospital in downtown Olympia, and one at a stand-alone center in Aberdeen, a timber community some 60 miles west of Olympia at Gray's Harbor.

Environmental Systems Research Institute. Inc.

Defining service areas

The first step in the process was to define the service areas of the existing dialysis facilities. Judging that people could reasonably be expected to drive twenty minutes to a dialysis facility, the Decision Support team used ArcView Network Analyst (an ArcView add-on product) to generate service areas that radiated outward from each center along major roads.

Creating a twenty-minute drive-time buffer (rather than a simple circle with a 20-mile radius) produced the two green polygons in the map at the right. Since people must use roads to get to a dialysis center, this method gave a realistic picture of accessibility.

ArcView Network Analyst uses the "Seconds" field in a database of major roads to calculate service areas. The "Seconds" data (which specifies, in seconds, how long it takes to drive along each section of road) is derived by dividing the length of the road segment by the speed limit.

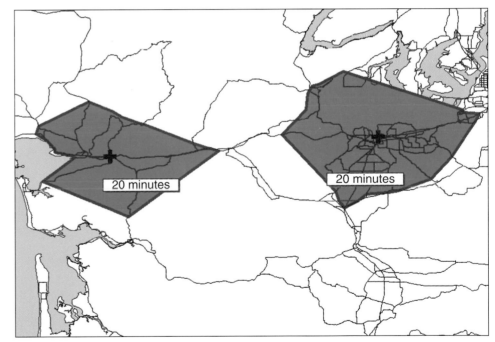

The green polygons cover the areas within a twenty-minute drive of a St. Peter Hospital dialysis center.

Looking at current demand

With patient data provided by the Northwest Renal Network, analysts next created a color-coded map showing by ZIP Code the number of people needing hemodialysis. The areas shown in dark green have the most patients.

By adding the twenty-minute drive-time polygons to the map, analysts saw that the existing centers were well-placed to meet current need. The dark green areas extending outside the red polygons belong to large ZIP Codes that range into largely rural areas; the bulk of the population in these ZIP Codes lives within the twenty-minute service areas.

But what would the future hold? To answer this question, Decision Support next looked at projected five-year population growth to see whether, and where, any new centers would need to be opened.

Data acquired from a public agency was used to create this map of dialysis patients by ZIP Code in the five-county area.

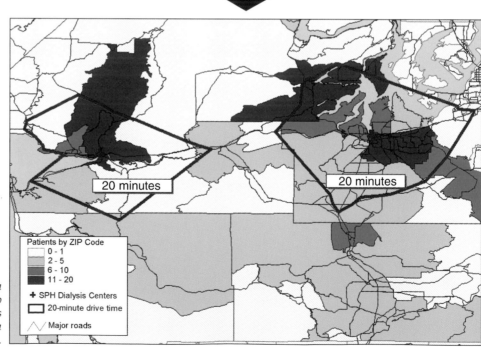

Zip	Name	Dialysis Patients
98503	OLYMPIA	19
98520	ABERDEEN	13
98501	OLYMPIA	13
98584	SHELTON	12
98513	OLYMPIA	11
98506	OLYMPIA	8
98502	OLYMPIA	8
98531	CENTRALIA	7
98550	HOQUIAM	7

Dialysis Patients by ZIP Code

Patients by ZIP Code
- 0 - 1
- 2 - 5
- 6 - 10
- 11 - 20
+ SPH Dialysis Centers
□ 20-minute drive time
/\/ Major roads

20 minutes

20 minutes

Estimating future demand

Like many parts of the Pacific Northwest, the greater Olympia region is projected to grow rapidly through the rest of the decade. In order to determine the best site for the next St. Peter dialysis center, the analysts looked at data that projected population growth between 1996 and 2001.

This time they worked at the census block group level to create a detailed picture of growth in the area.

When the data was mapped in ArcView GIS, it showed the population increasing sharply in the area around and to the south of Olympia. Stable or even declining population was projected for areas to the west.

Shape	Block Group ID	1996 Pop	2001 Pop	% Growth
Polygon	530530625.006	601	656	0.09
Polygon	530530625.007	961	1026	0.07
Polygon	530530625.008	1152	1287	0.12
Polygon	530530626.001	705	762	0.08
Polygon	530530626.002	369	395	0.07
Polygon	530530626.003	708	768	0.08
Polygon	530530627.001	272	323	0.19
Polygon	530530627.002	788	834	0.06
Polygon	530530627.003	105	102	-0.03
Polygon	530530628.011	1466	1700	0.16
Polygon	530530628.012	1441	1687	0.17
Polygon	530530628.013	3690	4349	0.18

Projected Population Growth by Block Group

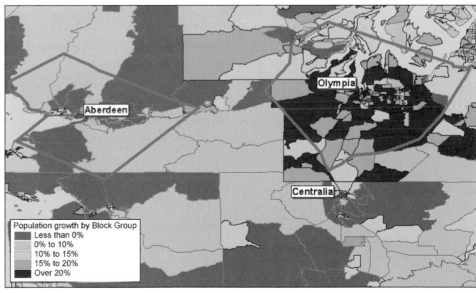

Population growth by Block Group
- Less than 0%
- 0% to 10%
- 10% to 15%
- 15% to 20%
- Over 20%

This color-coded map of census block groups shows that the highest population growth will occur around Olympia. Rural areas nearer the coast will hold constant or lose population.

Locating a new site

The final step in the project was to select the census block groups that lay *outside* the existing twenty-minute service areas, and then rank these according to projected five-year population growth. This would give St. Peter management an idea of where to begin planning for a future facility.

The analysis identified the four fastest-growing block groups that were more than twenty minutes from an existing center. Tellingly, these areas were all clustered around the community of Centralia, south of Olympia.

The findings were well received by management. Decision Support had established that current facilities were, in fact, well placed to meet demand. Furthermore, the analysis revealed an area north of Centralia that should be the first place to consider putting a new dialysis center (and other facilities as well).

In this case, ArcView GIS delivered a clear presentation of the facts.

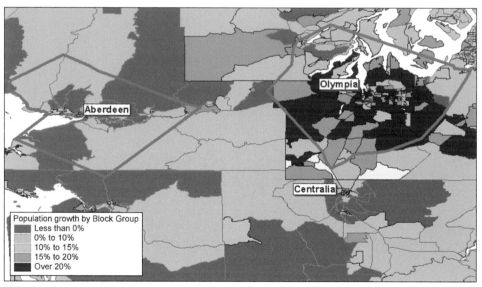

The census block groups highlighted in yellow are the fastest-growing ones that lie outside existing dialysis service areas.

Data

Five-year projected population growth by block group provided by Equifax National Decision Systems, San Diego, California.

Major roads layer and detailed counties data from *Data and Maps* CD–ROM (included with ArcView GIS), ESRI.

Software

ArcView GIS for Windows

ArcView Network Analyst for Windows

Acknowledgments

Thanks to Doug Upson of the Decision Support Group of Providence/St. Peter Hospital.

**Providence/
St. Peter Hospital**

Making maps for marketing communication

Cartography, the art and science of producing maps, has been revolutionized by GIS technology. Many atlases, street guides, and other maps that used to be painstakingly drawn by experts are now created and edited digitally. With the advent of affordable desktop GIS and commercial data, high-quality maps can now be made by ordinary businesspeople and either printed directly or integrated with desktop publishing documents.

In this chapter, you'll see how a small expedition outfitter used ArcView GIS and inexpensive, off-the-shelf geographic data to create maps for its promotional materials.

Marketing on a minimum

UltraMarine Sea Kayaking (Santa Cruz, California) is a two-person company that organizes sea kayak adventure vacations. With destinations ranging from Baja California in winter to the Pacific Northwest in summer, the owner-operators spend more than half their time conducting tours. The promotional materials describing their trips are UltraMarine's main sales tool while the owners are out of the office.

The format of their pieces has evolved from a black-and-white brochure to a full-color poster, produced in-house with ArcView GIS and standard desktop publishing software. The maps on the UltraMarine poster are both accurate and attractive—they present detailed information in a way that's vivid and easy to absorb and that excites customer interest in their unusual destinations.

Guided ocean-kayak vacationing is a popular segment of the adventure travel business. As travelers become more discerning and the number of vacation packages increases, outfitters are relying on better marketing materials to attract customers.

Assembling the data

The great advantage to using GIS for cartography is that the map files you need are readily available from commercial sources—so that drawing a map is as easy as double-clicking to open a file. Because these map files are professionally produced, detailed, and accurate, the businesses that use them to create marketing materials can relax and devote their energies to design.

Recently, UltraMarine prepared a poster for a four-day trip around the San Juan Islands in Washington State. The layout they wanted called for four different maps: a tour map showing a close-up of the kayak route, two locator maps to show how to get to the launch site, and a three-dimensional relief map of the islands.

The map files they needed (shown at the right) were easily obtained from a few different sources and loaded into ArcView GIS.

Geographic boundary and town location data came from ESRI's Digital Chart of the World. (All map files have associated database tables containing statistical information.)

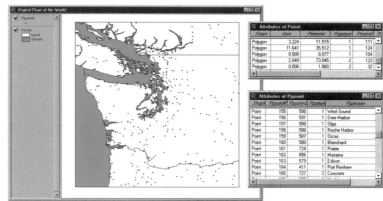

The free data that comes with ArcView GIS software included state boundaries and major roads.

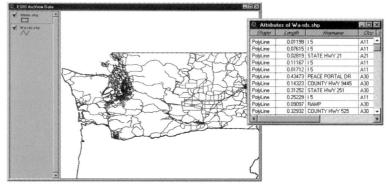

Elevation data compiled by the U.S. Geological Survey was purchased from a commercial vendor. It would be used to generate a 3-D relief map.

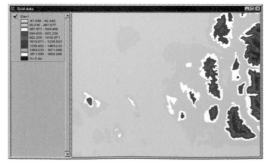

The tour map

The UltraMarine mapmakers found that ArcView GIS software made it easy to add and edit the data they wanted to use. They could set the map scale to any desired level of detail. ArcView also gave them full control over the color of each map element, the size and font of labels, and the choice of symbols used to represent particular features. These aspects of map design are collectively referred to as *symbology*.

The final tour map, shown at the right, uses bright colors sparingly. Dark blue markers indicate the nightly campsites, while the black line contrasts the kayak route with the blue of the water. Different text colors are used to distinguish island names, town names, and destination points. The scale bar and north arrow provide spatial orientation.

UltraMarine exported the map as a TIFF graphic file and brought it into a *PageMaker*® (Adobe Systems, Mountain View, California) document. This is where the new poster would begin to take shape.

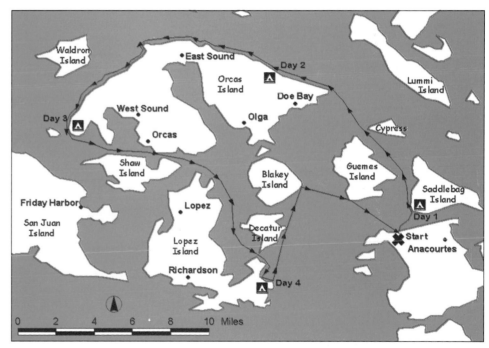

On the finished map, X marks the spot where the kayakers depart. The map succeeds thanks to the story it tells and its clean design.

The locator maps

The two locator maps put the San Juan Islands in geographic context. The smaller map shows the entire state of Washington and Puget Sound; a black rectangle defines the extent of the next map: a close-up view of the Bellingham area.

The same design principles used in the tour map apply to these maps, too: carefully chosen colors, line widths, and text fonts contribute to a clean, well-proportioned look. Special graphic symbols (included with ArcView GIS) identify state and

interstate highways as well as the two local airports.

Like the tour map, the locator maps were exported from ArcView in TIFF format, then imported into PageMaker.

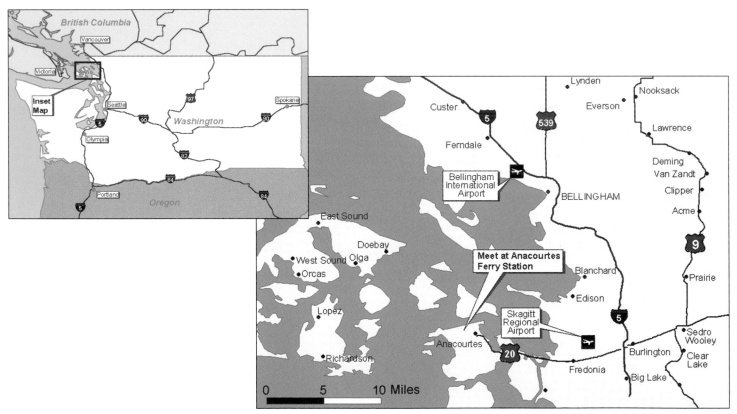

The two locator maps contain the same geographic data shown at different scales. The scale of a map determines the amount of detail shown.

The 3-D relief map

For added visual punch, UltraMarine decided to include a three-dimensional relief map of the area on their poster. Relief maps show elevation and other features of topography; they simulate what the earth would look like from an airplane.

Capitalizing on the ability of ArcView Spatial Analyst to interpret elevation data, the mapmakers generated a 3-D display from commercially available DTMs, or Digital Terrain Models. This data, collected by the U.S. Geological Survey, consists of elevation values for a number of sample points in a surveyed area. Based on the sample points, ArcView Spatial Analyst interpolates values for all points, thus creating a continuous surface in relief. The elevations at zero feet or below (the waters of Puget Sound) are shaded dark blue for visual contrast.

This file, like those before it, was exported as a TIFF image and added to the PageMaker document.

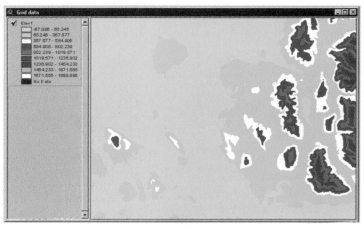

Elevation data was used to generate the 3-D relief map shown below.

The final product

EXPLORING THE SAN JUAN ISLANDS:
4-day Kayak Adventures

Experience the dramatic and wildlife-rich San Juan Islands from the ultimate perspective: a sea kayak. **By day,** see and photograph killer whales, minke whales, porpoises, bald eagles, and myriad bird life. **By night,** enjoy luxury camping complete with gourmet cooking and fine wines. We'll train you first, then spoil you, as you take in one of America's true natural wonders: the **San Juan Islands.**

How to get there

Where we'll be ▶

For information call

UltraMarine
SEA KAYAKING

1-408-425-8840

The final product combines the maps, a couple of photos, and a few lines of text to create an attractive and informative poster. It's lightweight, easy to mail, even suitable for framing. The file is printed to an inkjet printer for proofing, then transferred to a printing service bureau via the Internet. Film output will be used by an offset printer to reproduce the poster in quantity.

Data

1:24,000 elevation data for relief map provided by American Digital Cartography, Appleton, Wisconsin.

Detailed coastlines from Digital Chart of the World, ESRI.

Highways, airports, and populated places data from *Data and Maps* CD–ROM (included with ArcView GIS), ESRI.

Software

ArcView GIS for Windows

ArcView Spatial Analyst for Windows

Adobe® PageMaker for Windows

Acknowledgments

Thanks to Noel Benson and Deborah Bell of UltraMarine Sea Kayaking.

Managing commercial real estate

Commercial real estate investment companies—companies that recommend acquisitions and manage portfolios—rely on well-organized, well-integrated database systems to stay competitive. The most successful firms invest heavily in information technology that delivers the latest market data to their employees quickly and easily. And because real estate is by its nature geographical, GIS is increasingly finding its way into the information infrastructure (the "infostructure") of many of the nation's largest real estate investment companies.

In this chapter, you'll see how one commercial real estate investment firm uses ArcView GIS as the cornerstone of its new companywide Market Information System, and how an asset manager in New York used the system to make some crucial decisions about a property in Southern California.

Commercial real estate management

SSR Realty Advisors, Inc. (White Plains, New York), a subsidiary of The Metropolitan Life Insurance Company (New York, New York), is a commercial real estate investment firm that manages assets worth over $2.6 billion.

On behalf of its clients—foreign investors, foundations, and public and private pension funds—SSR Realty Advisors buys and sells apartment buildings, industrial complexes, offices, and shopping centers throughout the United States. The firm's success is measured largely by the returns it provides on these investments.

At any given time, SSR may be reviewing as many as 300 properties. Managing the portfolios (that is, buying and selling the right properties at the right time, and making sure they stay fully leased and well maintained) is no easy matter, so asset and acquisition managers rely on an extensive research database.

SSR Realty Advisors, Inc., uses ArcView GIS at its headquarters in White Plains, New York, to help manage its $2.6-billion commercial real estate portfolio.

GIS has proven successful in giving the firm's managers all the data they need (presented in the context of geography) to understand what's happening in markets that could be 3,000 miles away.

Integrating a GIS into the database

The real estate industry has long used geographic information systems to study regional economic trends and to see where properties are in relation to their surroundings.

But SSR incorporated GIS into the architecture of its enterprisewide database, becoming one of the first investment management companies to organize its entire information system according to geography.

Everyone in the company—whether in acquisitions, asset management, or asset divestiture—now uses the same map-based interface to get to the information (and the tools) they need to do their jobs.

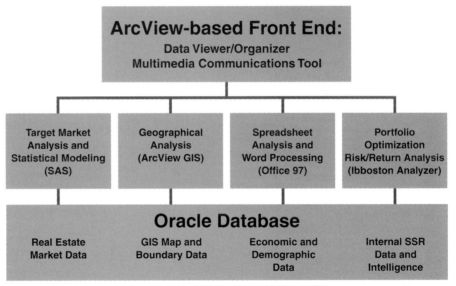

This chart depicts the structure of SSR's three-tiered Market Information System. From a common map-based interface, users can perform basic GIS analysis or get to other applications (like spreadsheets or word-processing templates).

The ArcView GIS interface

The user interface to the system is a customized version of ArcView GIS. The start-up screen displays a map of the United States with the 100 largest metropolitan areas drawn in pink. The interface also contains a toolbar for navigating the map and a set of buttons for accessing different parts of the system.

The interface gives all employees, regardless of their GIS experience, access to data according to location. They can easily get information about a place by clicking on it on the map; various buttons above the map take them to parts of the system designed for their particular needs.

So whether the task is to consider a new acquisition in Dallas, summarize the holdings of a client in Atlanta, or track the financial performance of a property in California, the SSR Market Information System makes it all happen within the same application.

When an asset manager at the company's headquarters had to find out how well a property in Southern California was doing, the system not only gave him the facts he needed, it supplied contextual information that helped him improve the property's performance. He began his review by clicking the Asset Management button on the main menu.

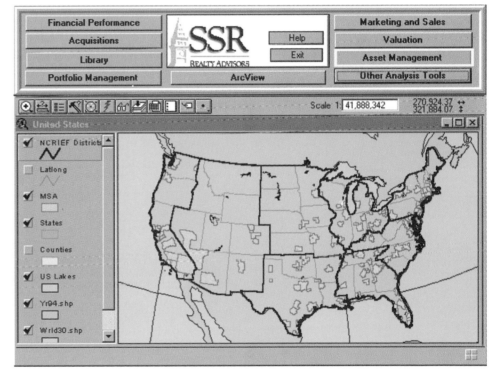

This screen is the main interface to the SSR Market Information System. It includes a map displaying the top 100 metropolitan markets in the United States, tools for navigating the map, and buttons that take the user to other parts of the system.

The Asset Management window

Clicking the Asset Management button brought the manager to a new window. Here the map looked slightly different: it still showed the continental United States and the major markets, but it also displayed points representing all properties currently managed by SSR. The points are color-coded according to property type (office buildings, retail, apartments, and so on).

When the manager clicked on the Orange County metropolitan area, the map zoomed in to Southern California. Additional features became visible—things like earthquake faults, toxic waste sites, freeways, and police and fire stations. Meanwhile, the state and metropolitan area boundaries—extraneous at the new scale—disappeared. This scale-dependent visibility keeps the map clean and focused on the appropriate data.

Next, the manager selected his name from the scrolling list at the top of the screen. This would filter the display so that only properties under his management would be seen.

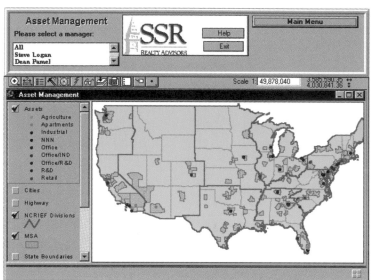

The manager selects what he wants to see next by clicking on a specific part of the country.

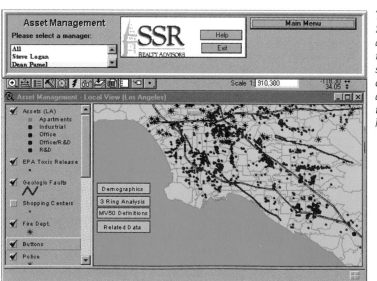

The local map of Southern California displays data that is relevant at this scale. The manager can now restrict the display to show just the properties he himself manages.

The new window showed a map of the assets under the manager's control, along with a set of buttons related to his specific duties—lease status, cash flow, property performance, and so on.

By clicking on the Property Performance button, he started a process that compared the performance of his properties to a national benchmark of similar properties. The results were automatically color-coded (black for profits, red for losses) and scaled according to the size of the profit or loss. In this way, he could easily see which properties were performing well and which needed attention.

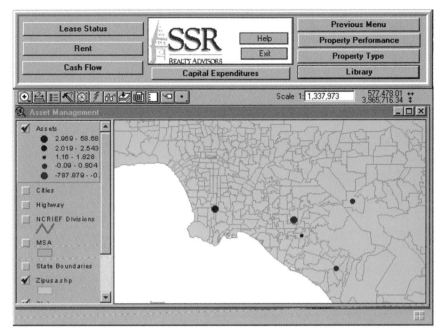

Scaled symbols convey the difference between properties performing at or above expectations (black dots) and those performing below expectations (red dots).

Looking at a property

Each dot symbol on the map is linked to a database that contains complete information about the property. The asset manager simply clicked on the red dot representing one of the underperforming properties (a corporate office center in Laguna Hills) to bring up the pertinent financial data. He was also able to access visual content like an aerial photo, an image of the building, and a diagram of the floor plan.

This information acquainted him with the characteristics of the property itself. But because the property was performing below expectations, he also needed a more detailed look at the local economy. He got this by clicking on the Library button.

The manager pulled up a variety of information about a property, including financial data, photographs, and floor plans.

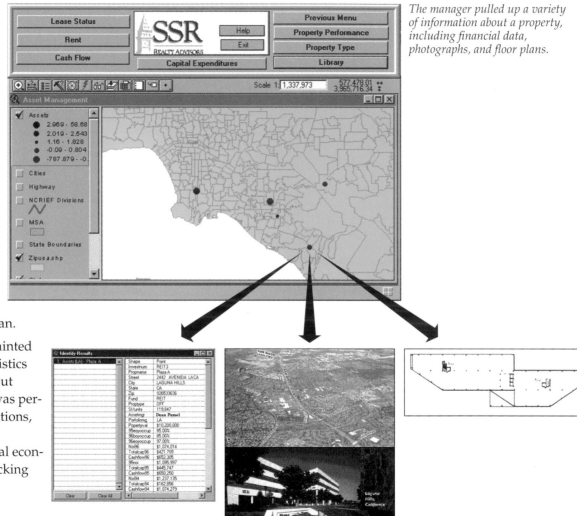

Checking the library

The asset manager was now presented with a window containing information about the regional economy and office vacancies in Southern California.

The new map showed a glut of corporate office space in the region, and a local economy still lagging behind the national economy in creating jobs. This led the manager to conclude that he needed to lower the price per square foot on the property in question or offer other incentives to find occupants for the complex.

The Market Information System provided the manager with a "virtual presence" in Southern California. With a few simple mouse clicks, he was able to check the status of his properties, and marshall all the resources of a complex database to act quickly on a problem.

In the larger scheme of things, SSR's use of GIS has earned the company a reputation as an innovator. Investors often cite the firm's leading-edge technology as a key reason for choosing it over competing investment companies.

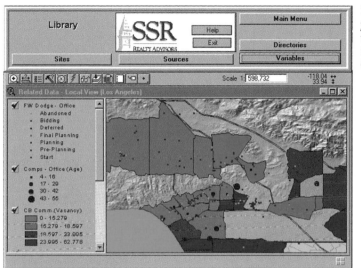

This map shows the percentage of office vacancies by census tract in the Southern California market.

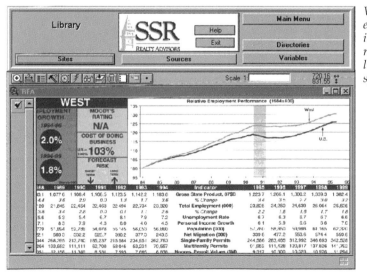

Various reports on economic trends and indicators can also be researched in the library section of the system.

Data

Highway data and state and county boundaries provided by Geographic Data Technology, Lyme, New Hampshire.

Benchmark comparisons provided by National Council of Real Estate Investment Fiduciaries (NCREIF).

Real estate market and other financial data courtesy of specialized providers.

Other geographic data from *Data and Maps* CD–ROM (included with ArcView GIS), ESRI.

Software

ArcView GIS for Windows

ArcView Dialog Designer for Windows (to create custom button interface)

Acknowledgments

Thanks to Fred Lieblich, Managing Director, and Lijian Chen, Research Manager, of SSR Realty, Inc.

Thanks as well to Gilbert Castle of Castle Consulting, San Francisco, California.

Environmental Systems Research Institute, Inc.

Tracking vehicles automatically

Companies that move people and products want to know where their vehicles are at any given moment. Radio communications help, but real-time tracking—that is, the ability to display a vehicle on a map at the same time that it's driving down the road—promises dramatic improvements in the areas of dispatching, route analysis, and driver safety. The technology has been on the horizon for some time, and now, with the commercial deployment of global positioning systems (which use satellites to fix the location of objects on the ground), it has finally arrived. Real-time vehicle tracking is now within reach of almost any business enterprise.

In this chapter, you'll see how the world's largest mail carrier tracks its postal vehicles in real time with GPS and ArcView GIS.

Improving delivery service

The United States Postal Service (USPS) runs the largest fleet of delivery vehicles in the world. Since 1971, the USPS has operated as a quasi-private agency, and it posted $1.6 billion in net income for fiscal year 1996. *Fortune Magazine* ranked the USPS thirty-third on its 1995 Global 500 list of the world's largest industrial and service corporations.

As part of its commitment to improve service through technology, the postal service launched a system in 1996 that they call GPSD, or Global Positioning System for Delivery. Introduced as a pilot program in Arlington, Texas, and elsewhere, the system has enabled the test sites to track their vehicles in real time, keep a record of where each vehicle has been, and provide mail carriers with an added measure of personal safety.

The United States Postal Service delivery fleet comprises over 200,000 vehicles, including these GPS-equipped trucks used by the Arlington, Texas, post office.

How the technology works

To track a vehicle in real time, you have to be able to find out where it is at any given moment. That's what GPS technology is all about. The Global Positioning System is a constellation of twenty-four satellites launched by the U.S. government that orbit the earth at very high altitude. Using these satellites as reference points, a GPS receiver can determine its exact location anywhere on earth and record that location as a pair of latitude/longitude coordinates.

But GPS is just the starting point. To implement real-time tracking for its pilot sites, the USPS chose the *Automated Vehicle Location (AVL)* package from Radio Satellite Integrators, Inc. (Torrance, California).

Installed in each postal vehicle is a GPS receiver, a communications controller, a modem, and a radio. The communications controller collects information from the GPS and transmits a modem signal by radio to a computer (called a base station) at the post office.

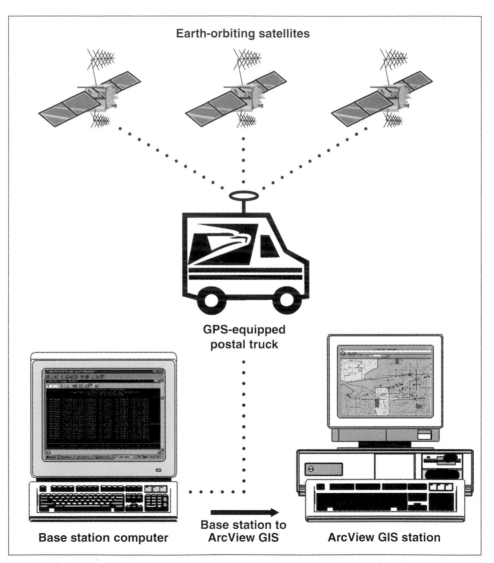

Earth-orbiting satellites

GPS-equipped postal truck

Base station computer

Base station to ArcView GIS

ArcView GIS station

The complete Automated Vehicle Location system includes the hardware in the vehicles, the base and GIS computers, and the software.

The GPS data comes into the base station as a list of readings, each of which includes the truck's latitude, longitude, speed, and direction; the status of the mail carrier (walking the route, on break); and the time the reading was taken. In the event of an emergency, the postal worker can also send a distress signal by pressing a "panic button" installed in the truck. This causes an alarm to sound and makes the screen on the base station computer flash yellow. The promise of increasing the safety of carriers has been one of the main forces behind automated vehicle tracking.

The base station computer removes errors and degradation in the signals, then converts them to a file in dBASE format. This file is then sent across a local area network to another computer running ArcView GIS. At this point, the file can be used to create a real-time display on a digital map.

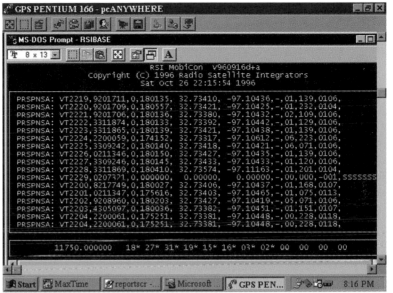

This is what the raw data from the trucks looks like when it's transmitted to the base station...

...and this is what it looks like after being converted to an ArcView GIS table in .dbf format. It can now be used to generate a real-time map display.

The real-time display

Back at the Arlington office, an employee monitors the current position of each vehicle on a digital map that's updated every thirty seconds. The system automatically places a numbered icon representing each truck in its correct position. The employee can see exactly where each truck is at any given time. The angle of the icon tells him which way the truck is going. Using a customized ArcView GIS interface, the employee can pan the display and zoom in or out, identify and label streets, find trucks by number, and measure distances.

If a carrier pushes the panic button in his truck, the map background flashes bright yellow, and the vehicle in question is highlighted and centered on the screen. Only when the operator confirms that the emergency has been resolved does the system return to normal status.

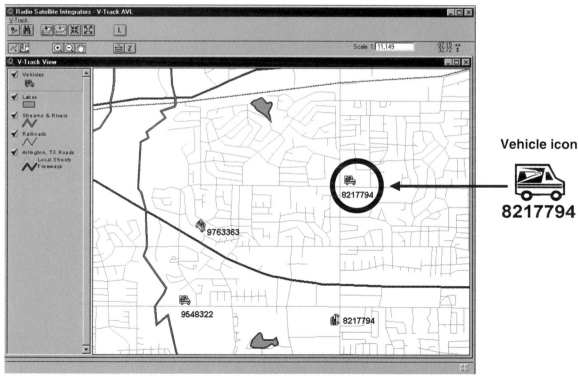

Vehicle icon

8217794

The real-time display is a customized ArcView GIS application programmed to update itself with new vehicle locations. The operator can toggle on or off various layers of data, including streets, landmarks, and ZIP Code boundaries.

Route analysis

The AVL system also simplifies route analysis. The USPS currently evaluates route performance at infrequent intervals, using a standard form known as a "3999." Before AVL, this form would be filled out by a supervisor who accompanied a carrier on her route for an entire day.

The main reason for evaluating route performance is to reduce "street time," or the amount of time that a carrier spends delivering the mail. Street time constitutes the single largest expense for the USPS. Operations managers look at both the efficiency of the route (the amount of driving required relative to the number of addresses), and at how quickly the carriers are delivering the mail.

With the AVL system, the data generated each day is stored in history databases. Using a simple electronic form, supervisors can automatically create maps like the one on this page for route evaluations, as well as the required 3999.

Because data is collected every day for every route, more complete information is available for analysis. And because the evaluations are generated automatically, supervisors no longer need accompany carriers.

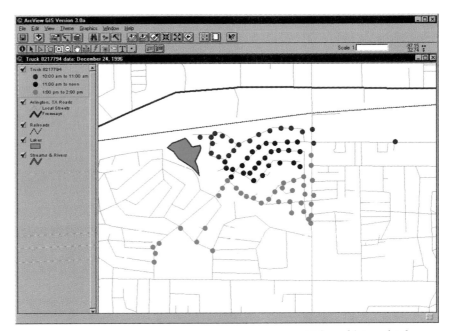

Using a history database generated from the vehicles' actual positions every day, the AVL can automatically generate maps like this one that are used to evaluate route efficiency.

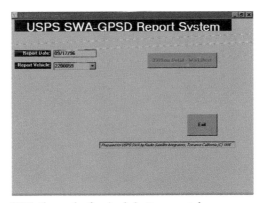

With the push of a single button, postal management can now generate a report that previously had to be written by a supervisor on the street.

The future

Based on the success of the Arlington pilot, and others, the USPS will be introducing the GPSD system in many more post offices over the next few years. Eventually, the system will include additional route management and evaluation tools, parcel tracking and tracing, two-way messaging for carrier-to-office communications, and regular maintenance of an already massive address database.

The USPS has embraced automated vehicle tracking as a way to help make sure the carrier on the street is safe, and going about his or her duties in the most efficient way possible. GIS is an integral part of the technology.

Data

Street data provided by Etak, Menlo Park, California.

ZIP Code boundaries data from *Data and Maps* CD–ROM (included with ArcView GIS), ESRI.

Software

ArcView GIS for Windows

Fontographer® for Windows by Macromedia® (San Francisco, California) used to create postal truck icon

Acknowledgments

Thanks to the United States Postal Service, Southwest Area.

Thanks, also, to Mark Holzworth of Radio Satellite Integrators, Inc.

Delivering interactive maps on the Web

In less than a decade, the World Wide Web (the multimedia part of the Internet) has done more to change the nature of business communication than any technology since the telephone. On the "Web," as it's now known, businesses can provide information to customers anywhere on earth, any time of day. When that information has a spatial dimension, there is no better tool for accessing it than a map.

In this chapter, you'll see how a major software company uses ArcView GIS and ArcView Internet Map Server software to create electronic dealer referral maps for the Internet-connected public.

ESRI: The GIS People

Environmental Systems Research Institute, Inc. (Redlands, California), is the market and technical leader in the multibillion-dollar geographic information systems industry.

The company began in 1969 as a consulting firm; along the way, it began developing software for in-house use. In the 1980s, ESRI released its first full-fledged commercial GIS software product, ARC/INFO, and it has continued to develop the most widely used GIS programs in the world. With the sudden explosion of the World Wide Web, ESRI developed a set of Internet Map Server products— technology that promises a whole new realm of business opportunities and improved customer service by putting GIS on the Web.

Using ArcView Internet Map Server software, ESRI has implemented its own Web-based application designed to help customers locate the GIS expert nearest them.

ESRI headquarters in Redlands, California. ESRI created a Web-based application that helps users find the nearest (and most suitable) dealer, developer, or consultant.

The case for Web-based information

The Internet is now the world's information supermarket. Businesses large and small, mainstream and specialized, have found it an ideal medium for projecting their corporate identities and offering a wide range of information. From a company's "home page," users can connect to all kinds of services—text and image-based data, product descriptions and demos, searchable databases, downloadable software, and more. Web-browsing software (like Netscape™ or Microsoft Internet Explorer) is now used by more people than any other PC software, and this helps explain why it's nearly impossible to find a major company without an extensive Web site.

The advantages the Internet offers are enormous. From the consumer's point of view, access to information is immediate and available around the clock. Not only that, but it's relatively easy to find what you're looking for (no misdirected transfers or voicemail dead ends). From the business angle, the system can be updated quickly and without reliance on third-party vendors, such as print shops. As the technology becomes ever more important, it's also becoming faster and more sophisticated, able to deliver increasingly complex services.

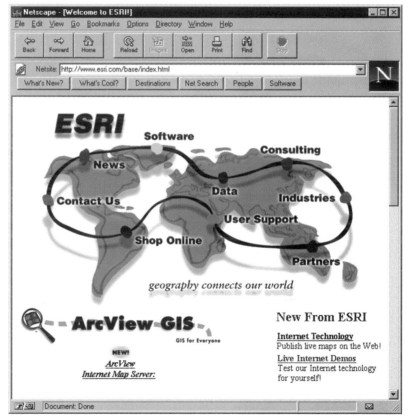

The ESRI home page. ESRI uses this site (www.esri.com) to make information available to its user community. Among the resources are product information, downloadable scripts, and links to other GIS sites. Clicking on the word "Partners" on the home page allows the user to access an ArcView GIS application that locates ESRI resellers and consultants.

How the Web works

The Internet is the world's largest computer network. Any two computers connected to it can communicate with one another and share information. While a variety of Internet services are in use (e-mail, ftp, newsgroups, chat), the most widely used is the World Wide Web. In fact, people often think the Web *is* the Internet.

In a few words, here's how the Web works. Any information stored in digital form (text, graphics, pictures, sound, and more) can be placed on a specially configured computer known as a "Web server." Individual computers ("clients") are then able to connect to that server through the Internet and access its information. A visual interface lets users move to different "pages" on a Web site, or to different Web sites altogether, by clicking on special buttons known as links.

Current technology makes it possible to put entire software programs on a Web server and run them *from* the client machine *on* the server machine. (To the user, it looks as if it were all happening on her own computer.) And this is where ArcView Internet Map Server enters the picture.

Links on the ESRI home page take the user to different parts of the Web site, including areas where she can purchase products online or download free data.

ArcView Internet Map Server

ArcView Internet Map Server is a product that allows a computer to be a Web server for GIS software applications. What this means is that a customized ArcView GIS program can be loaded on a server and used by anyone on the Internet. At ESRI, one computer is the main Web server (containing company news, product information, and so on), and another computer, connected to it, is a dedicated map application server.

The possibilities created by ArcView Internet Map Server are extraordinary. Any information a business might want to display in map form can now be accessed by anyone in the world. Even more importantly, these maps can be made interactive—that is, they can be part of a software application running on the business's Web server. It follows that all the tools of a full-featured GIS can be made available, including the ability to zoom in and out and pan the display, to search for specific locations by various criteria, and to determine spatial relationships, such as the distance from one city to another.

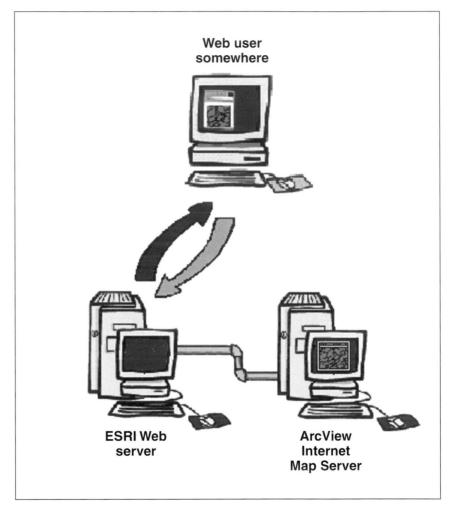

Web user somewhere

ESRI Web server

ArcView Internet Map Server

A user who connects to ESRI's Web site can link to an ArcView GIS application that finds ESRI resellers and consultants and displays their locations on a map. The fact that the application is running on a remote computer makes no difference to the user: she interacts with it as if it were a program on her own machine.

Environmental Systems Research Institute, Inc.

Business Partner Locator

A good example of map server technology at work is Business Partner
Locator, a customized ArcView GIS
application that can be accessed from
ESRI's Web site. Dealer referral services are offered by many companies—usually you call an 800 number
and provide your ZIP Code. A customer service rep sorts a reseller database on the ZIP Code field and gives
you a location in your area. But when
a service like this is presented as a GIS
application on the Web, it saves the
customer time and the company man-
power—and delivers a lot more information in the bargain.

The interface to Business Partner
Locator displays a map of the United
States. The locations of ESRI business
partners (resellers, consultants, data
vendors, and developers) are shown as
colored symbols; major highways are
drawn in red. The user has two ways
to zero in on her area of interest: enter
a ZIP Code and click the Go Find It!
button, or navigate and zoom using
the tools at the top of the display.

Suppose a user in Houston, Texas,
wants to find a business partner in
her area. She decides to enter her
ZIP Code to bring up a more
detailed map.

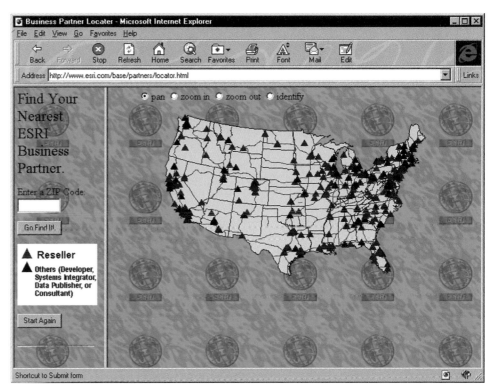

From the main interface, the user can zoom in on any part of the country.

The Results window

After clicking the Go Find It! button, the user is presented with a map centered on the midpoint of the ZIP Code she entered. Surrounding this point is a series of 5-, 10-, and 20-mile-radius rings. Also shown are local interstate highways and, of course, all the business partners in the area.

If she wants, the user can zoom in still further with the navigation tools, but, in this case, the level of detail is sufficient. Looking for a reseller of ESRI software, she selects the "identify" tool at the top of the display, then clicks on the triangle closest to the center of the rings.

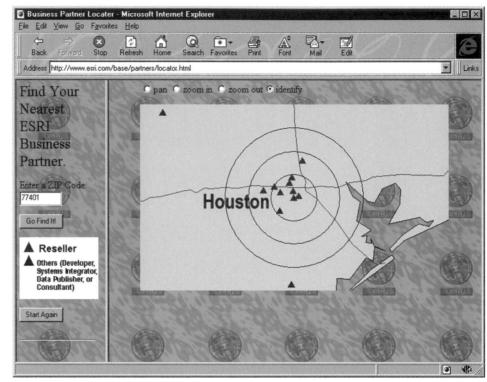

The Results window shows a map of the Houston area, with 5-, 10-, and 20-mile-radius rings around the selected ZIP Code.

Identifying a business partner

Clicking on the symbol brought up a profile of the business partner located there. The profile data resides in a database linked to the application, and includes name and address information and a description of services offered.

If the business partner has its own Web site, the URL field in the profile will contain a link directly to the partner's home page.

To see this application in action, just point your Web browser to www.esri.com and go to the section labeled "Partners" on the main ESRI page.

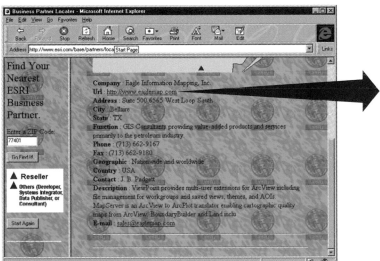

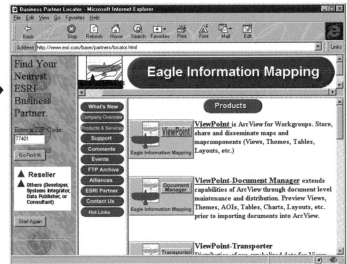

After clicking on a business partner, the user is presented with a screen of information and a link to the partner's home page.

Data

State boundaries, interstate highways, and city locations from data included with ArcView GIS.

Software

ArcView GIS for Windows

ArcView Internet Map Server

Acknowledgments

Thanks to Matt McGunigle of ESRI.

Environmental Systems Research Institute, Inc.

Getting GIS data for business applications

All GIS analysis (all analysis, for that matter) begins at the same point: you need to know what you need to know. The process of answering this question inevitably leads you to make decisions about the information that is relevant to your task. For this reason, it can be said that data is at the heart of every GIS project.

Depending on the data you presently maintain (in databases, spreadsheets, or other files), you may already have much of what you need on hand. Usually, however, you'll have to obtain at least some information from outside sources. The purpose of this chapter is to acquaint you with some of the most useful data that the GIS community makes available and to point you to some of its leading vendors. First, however, it will be helpful to briefly introduce the two main categories of data used in a GIS.

Spatial and attribute data

A GIS integrates two fundamentally different types of data. One type defines the shape and location of places—this is called *spatial* data. The other type describes those places, and the people who live in them and the things that happen there—this is called *attribute* data. Put succinctly, spatial data enables you to draw a map; attribute data makes the map meaningful.

Although they are structurally different, spatial and attribute data live symbiotically in a GIS, and it's hard to talk about one apart from the other.

The map files you get from commercial (and noncommercial) sources normally include both. This chapter treats spatial data first and attribute data afterward, but the separation, while clear in theory, is taxing to maintain in practice, and each type will therefore be discussed to some extent in terms of the other.

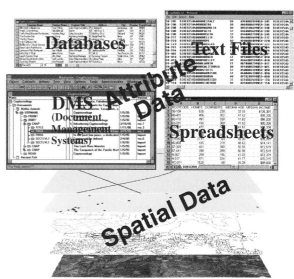

Vector, raster, and image data

Spatial data itself can be divided into three types. The type most common in GIS (especially in business GIS) is called *vector* data. Vector data represents geographic features as either points, lines, or polygons. Polygons tend to be used for sizable areas like countries or ZIP Codes; lines for things like streets and rivers; and points to represent specific locations, like businesses. (The shape used to represent a particular feature may depend on the scale of the map.)

Raster data takes a different approach to the mapping problem by dividing geographic space into a matrix of identically-sized cells. Each cell is linked to a number that stands for some geographical property (for example, "1" for land, "2" for sea, and "3" for shore). To illustrate the difference, a road in a vector data map might be drawn as a line of a particular width and length. The same road in a raster data map would consist of a string of adjacent cells, each with the same value (say "4"). For the purposes of analogy, you might think of a vector data map as a pen drawing and a raster data map as a tile mosaic.

This map of the United States was created with vector data. State capitals are represented as points, interstate highways as lines, and state boundaries as polygons.

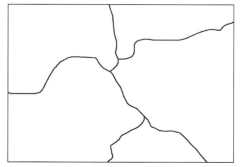 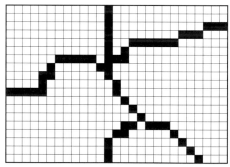

In these maps, the same highways are depicted as a vector data structure on the left, and a raster data structure on the right.

The third type of spatial data is *image* data, which includes such things as satellite and aerial photographs, and optically scanned paper maps. Strictly speaking, image data is a kind of raster data, because an image is composed of uniformly-sized cells (pixels) linked to specific numbers—numbers that represent a color or grayness value. Image data can serve as a visual backdrop to vector data. It can also be used to create vector data through a digital tracing process, or even for analysis in a discipline known as *remote sensing*.

ArcView GIS uses vector spatial data (the kind of data predominantly featured in the case studies in this book); it can also display image data. ArcView Spatial Analyst is a raster-based product that integrates seamlessly with ArcView GIS. It allows you to analyze raster data and to convert raster data to vector data.

By now, you may know more than you ever wanted to about spatial data types, but this information could be useful down the road. The rest of the chapter is a survey of data sets (both spatial and attribute) that GIS professionals find valuable.

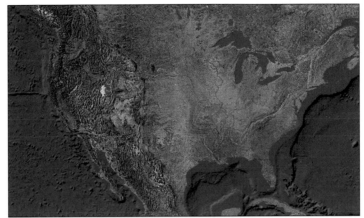

This cloud-free satellite image of the United States from WorldSat (Mississauga, Ontario) is actually a carefully matched quiltwork of images taken at different times. The ocean floor was imaged with traditional sonar.

The latest satellites are capable of delivering 5-meter- and 1-meter-resolution images, like these of San Francisco from SpaceImaging Corp. (Thornton, Colorado).

Vector spatial data

Postal geography

U.S. five-digit ZIP Codes are widely used in business and marketing applications. A complete map file of these ZIP Codes is included with ArcView GIS.

A less commonly used designation is the three-digit ZIP Code. Direct mail firms operating at the national level often work with three-digit ZIP Codes because data management is easier—there are 886 zones instead of 40,000—and because three-digit codes still conform to USPS presorting (discounting) routines.

The most detailed level of postal geography is the ZIP+4. In fact, ZIP+4 locations are so specific they can only be shown as points. They may represent places as particular as one side of a city block or a single floor of a large office complex. ZIP+4 files are useful for displaying the distribution of customer or vendor locations.

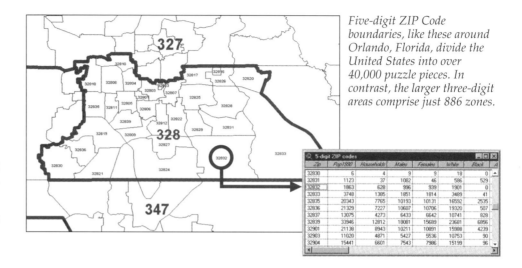

Five-digit ZIP Code boundaries, like these around Orlando, Florida, divide the United States into over 40,000 puzzle pieces. In contrast, the larger three-digit areas comprise just 886 zones.

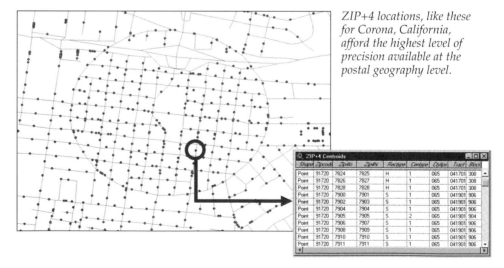

ZIP+4 locations, like these for Corona, California, afford the highest level of precision available at the postal geography level.

Environmental Systems Research Institute, Inc.

Census geography

The U.S. Census Bureau reports statistics from the decennial census, along with other research, according to the following units: state, county, tract, block group, and block. Census geography is the closest thing to a standard reporting system in the GIS data industry: almost all vendors supply information organized by one or more of the Bureau's geographic designations.

Census tracts are relatively stable statistical subdivisions of a county. They include from 2,500 to 8,000 people and average around 4,000. Census tracts usually follow visible features (like roads or rivers), and are always completely contained within county lines. At the tract level, the Census Bureau reports its full range of demographic statistics, including income, race, age, and much more.

Block groups are clusters of blocks within the same census tract. They are the smallest units for which detailed statistics are released.

The block is the smallest geographic unit recognized by the Bureau. Census blocks are areas bounded by four or more streets. Because a block may contain just a single household, privacy issues dictate that this data consist only of population and number of households.

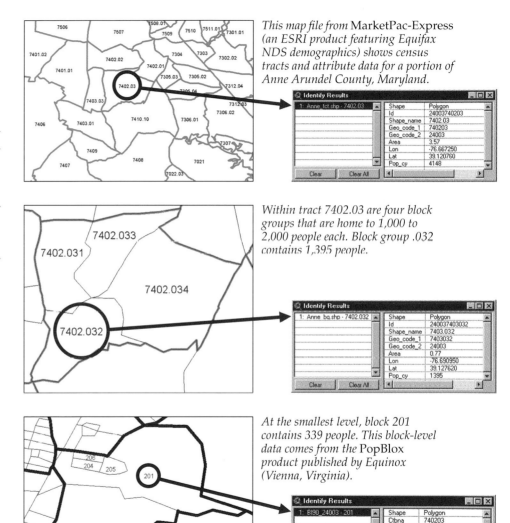

This map file from MarketPac-Express *(an ESRI product featuring Equifax NDS demographics) shows census tracts and attribute data for a portion of Anne Arundel County, Maryland.*

Within tract 7402.03 are four block groups that are home to 1,000 to 2,000 people each. Block group .032 contains 1,395 people.

At the smallest level, block 201 contains 339 people. This block-level data comes from the PopBlox *product published by Equinox (Vienna, Virginia).*

Parcel geography

Used primarily by the real estate industry, parcel geography displays individual pieces of property, along with information about their value, ownership, and lending and transaction history.

The sample on this page from Transamerica Information Management (Irvine, California) shows a portion of Santa Clara, California.

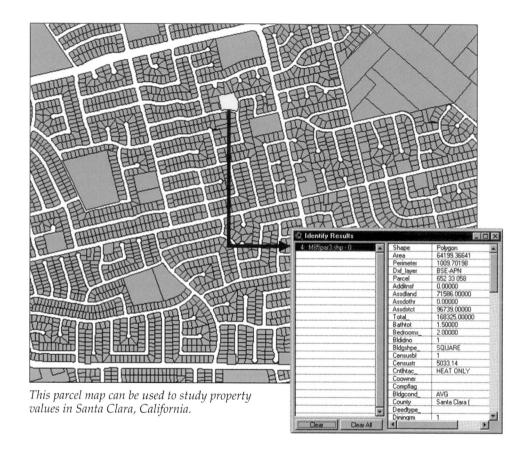

This parcel map can be used to study property values in Santa Clara, California.

Television and media markets

Areas of Dominant Influence (ADIs) and Metropolitan Statistical Areas (MSAs) divide the United States into specialized geographic subregions.

ADIs comprise 211 non-overlapping television markets. Determined by terrain, signal strength, and television-watching habits, these areas do not respect administrative boundaries such as state or county lines. Buyers of television commercial time rely heavily on data reported at the ADI level to target national broadcast campaigns.

MSAs are defined as core urban areas that contain a large population nucleus, together with adjacent communities having a high degree of economic and social integration with that core. Unlike ADIs, MSAs do not blanket the entire U.S. landmass. In fact, these 315 markets, which contain 80 percent of the nation's population, cover just 20 percent of the ground. Widely used in marketing research to support national advertising decisions, MSAs are a standard for comparing national markets with one another.

The ADI and MSA boundaries (along with their associated attributes) are included with ArcView GIS.

ADIs define the nation's 211 local television markets.

Almost 200 million Americans live in one of 315 MSAs. These markets represent the core of the nation's urban population.

Telecommunications

Telecommunications data, once employed only by telephone companies for logistical work, is now widely used thanks to industry deregulation and the hundreds of companies competing in telecommunications markets.

Telecommunications map files show things like cellular coverage areas, exchange and prefix codes, microwave transmitter locations, and cable television franchise regions. Local Access Transport Areas (LATAs) are used by long-distance carriers as a framework for building local and long-distance rate schedules.

The data on this page comes from On Target Mapping (Pittsburgh, Pennsylvania).

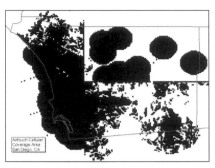

This map displays cellular coverage areas for San Diego, California.

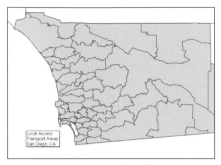

LATAs (shown here for San Diego) are used to determine whether a telephone call is local or long-distance.

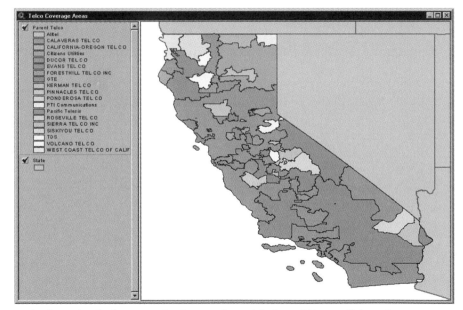

In the deregulated telecommunications markets of the late 1990s, conditions change quickly. GIS is the ideal way to access and update data of such a dynamic nature. This map shows the markets served by each of the twenty local companies now in the telephone business in California.

Roads and highways

Roads and highways are used to plan travel routes and to evaluate the accessibility of locations. In addition, they help place other map features (like business establishments) in a recognizable geographic context.

ArcView GIS comes with several important road and highway files (see the list at the end of this chapter). The file of U.S. interstate highways, for example, provides useful orientation for maps drawn at the national and state levels. ArcView Network Analyst software can be used with length and speed-limit data to plan coast-to-coast routes. (ArcView Network Analyst is a software extension that solves routing problems.)

A more detailed roads file may include not only interstate highways, but also noninterstates and major thoroughfares.

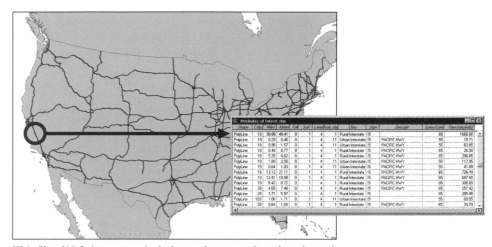

This file of U.S. interstates includes road segment length and speed limit fields useful for calculating driving time from one place to another.

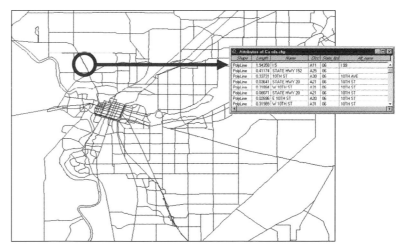

More detailed road files, as in this map of Sacramento, California, include major arterials, highways, and freeways, but exclude smaller residential streets.

Streets

Map files that include every known street in an area, from the twelve-lane superhighway to the narrowest residential road, play a special role in GIS applications. Because these files are theoretically complete, and contain address information for every block of every street, they are often used as base maps in geocoding.

The U.S. Census Bureau's TIGER/Line file was the first digital database of U.S. streets. The TIGER/Line remains useful for many basic GIS applications because it's an inexpensive source of detailed information. Since 1988, the Bureau has released several improved versions of the TIGER/Line file. Major enhancements to the 1995 version corrected address information and added ZIP+4 fields.

Enhanced TIGER/Line data, like the *Dynamap/2000* file shown here from Geographic Data Technology (Lyme, New Hampshire), contains up-to-date corrections of street networks required for routing applications.

These map files include a variety of local features (for instance, railroads, airports, churches, schools, public buildings, hospitals, and bodies of water) that add helpful orientation to map displays.

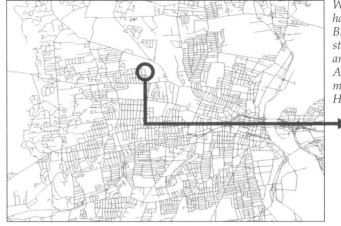

Wessex (Winnetka, Illinois) has taken the U.S. Census Bureau's current national street file (TIGER/Line 95) and converted it to an ArcView-ready format. This map shows the streets of Hartford, Connecticut.

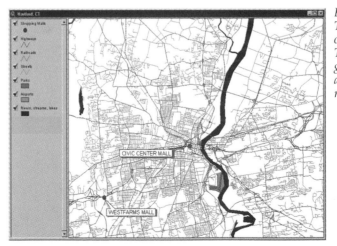

Enhanced versions of the TIGER/Line file, like this one from Geographic Data Technology, are useful for geocoding customer addresses and for creating richly-detailed maps.

Specialized streets and roads

The highest quality street files are fully navigable digital databases like the product from NavTech (Sunnyvale, California) shown at the right. To be navigable, a street database must list everything that affects how a street is driven, including such attributes as turn restrictions, one-way access, school zones, toll status, number of lanes, speed limit, and average actual speed. Navigable databases also boast extremely high positional accuracy and resolution, making them suitable for the most advanced transportation applications, like in-vehicle route guidance or emergency dispatch operations.

Highway volume data, like that shown below from Business Location Research (Tucson, Arizona) provides twenty-four-hour average daily traffic counts for U.S. interstates. Volume data is available for minor highways and arterials as well. This information might be an important factor in selecting a site for a new business.

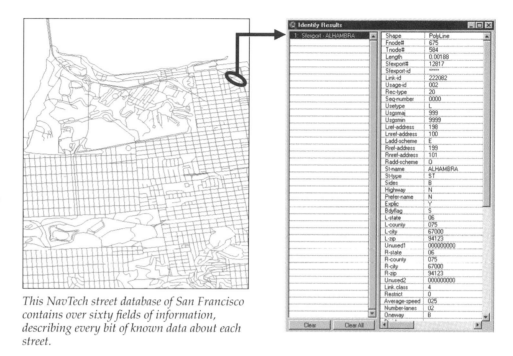

This NavTech street database of San Francisco contains over sixty fields of information, describing every bit of known data about each street.

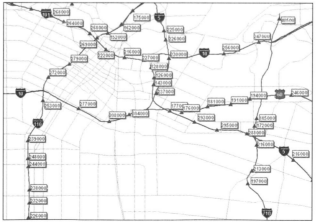

This network of freeways around Los Angeles logs some of the highest twenty-four-hour traffic volumes in the world.

Raster spatial data

Continuous-surface data

Raster data is useful in the display and analysis of geographic phenomena that change gradually over a surface, like population density, or the "gravity" with which a store attracts customers.

An extension product called ArcView Spatial Analyst is required to work with raster spatial data in ArcView GIS.

Another geographic property that can be represented with raster data is surface elevation. The 3-D relief map on this page, while resembling a satellite image, was actually generated from a file of surveyed elevation points (commonly known as a Digital Elevation Model, or DEM).

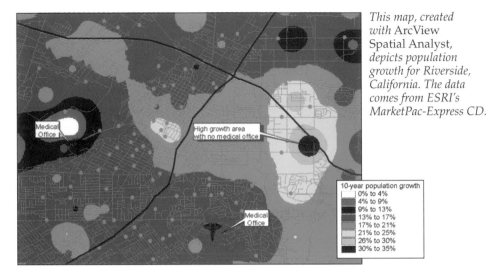

This map, created with ArcView Spatial Analyst, *depicts population growth for Riverside, California. The data comes from ESRI's MarketPac-Express CD.*

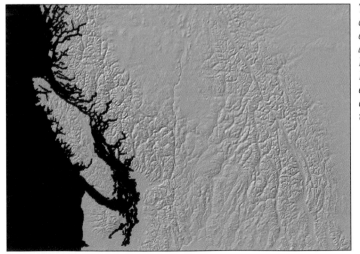

This TIFF image was created from a digital elevation model for the area around Vancouver, British Columbia. Elevation data for the entire North American continent is included with ArcView GIS.

Image spatial data

Satellite images and aerial photographs

One common source of image data is digital pictures of the earth's surface taken from earth-orbiting satellites (like the U.S. Landsat and the French SPOT).

High-resolution satellite images, besides being beautiful, have a number of applications in business GIS. Real estate developers use them to help plan new subdivisions because such images show what is really on the ground in a way no other data can. In general, satellite images can serve as visual backdrops for literally any vector GIS data, since by now the earth's surface has been completely photographed from space many times over.

Aerial photographs, because they are taken from a much lower altitude, can show more detail than satellite pictures (although the 1-meter-resolution satellite images soon to be commercially available will challenge that advantage). In a GIS, aerial photos can be a valuable tool for correcting existing vector data, or for creating new data through digital tracing.

This scene shows a 3-D perspective of Albertville, France (site of the 1992 Winter Olympics), that was used for logistical planning during the games. The image was created by extracting elevation data from a stereo pair of SPOT satellite images.

This aerial photo shows a small part of Olmstead County, Minnesota. The image, published by the U.S. Geological Survey, is so detailed that it depicts individual buildings and even the number of lanes on the freeway.

Relief maps and USGS quad sheets

Chalk Butte, Inc. (Boulder, Wyoming), uses elevation data to create three-dimensional full-color digital relief maps. The source data is DTM, or Digital Terrain Models, from the U.S. Geological Survey (USGS). These digital images can serve as detailed topographic base maps on which to overlay vector data.

The USGS publishes detailed paper maps, known as "quad sheets," that cover the entire United States.

A product called *Sure!Maps® Raster* from Horizons Technology (San Diego, California) is comprised of scanned versions of these maps. These digital quad sheets can be used in ArcView GIS to create new vector data or as visual backdrops.

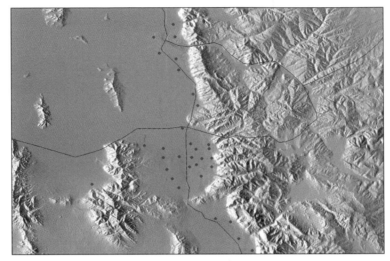

This color relief image of central Utah gives context to the vector data displayed on top of it. The lines represent major highways and the points populated places.

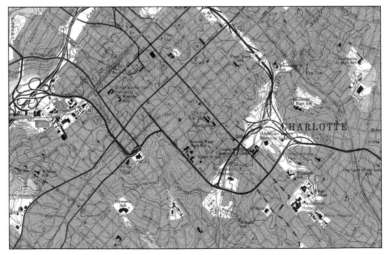

Charlotte, North Carolina, as depicted in a scanned USGS quad sheet.

Attribute data

Demographic updates and projections

Demographic forecasting is the science of analyzing population statistics and projecting trends. For socioeconomic information about Americans, the most reliable and detailed data is that collected once every ten years by the U.S. Census Bureau. The last full census was completed in 1990, so the work of forecasters becomes increasingly important as the decade winds down.

Projections are most commonly packaged as either current-year or five-year estimates. The map of California counties at the top of this page is colored to show median household income for the current year. The census tract map of Los Angeles County, bottom, shows which areas will see the largest percentage increase in the number of households over the next five years.

In fast-changing urban markets, having up-to-date and reliable projection data is essential for successful GIS analysis.

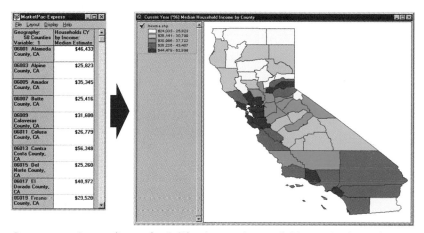

Current-year income figures for California counties, available on ESRI's MarketPac-Express CD, are actually projections of the 1990 census. The map is shaded from light to dark green to reflect median household income in each county.

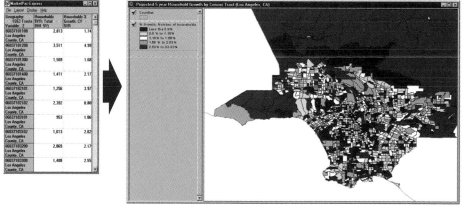

MarketPac-Express also includes five-year forecasts. This map shows the expected percentage increase in the number of households in Los Angeles County. Dark red areas are growing the fastest; dark blue areas will experience a decline.

Census attribute data

In addition to its pioneering efforts in the digital mapping of the nation's geography, the U.S. Census Bureau is also the country's largest collector and publisher of related attribute data. Most people know of the Bureau's massive decennial counting of U.S. population and housing. The summary tape files used to report census data are the basis for many of the forecasts offered by third-party data providers.

Since the late 1980s, the Bureau has been placing much of its content online at www.census.gov, where a vast amount of free information is now available. Many files can be viewed directly with standard Web browsers; other documents are available as downloadable PDF (Portable Document Format) files.

The table at right shows the number of insured banks per state, as well as the total assets and deposits maintained by all banks in each state. With minimal effort, this data can be dropped into a spreadsheet, exported to ArcView GIS, and linked with a state boundary file to create a color-coded map of commercial banking activity.

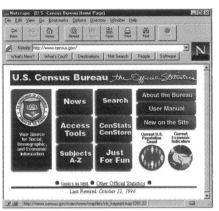

Industrial Reports
Education
Geography
Housing and Housing Starts
Income and Labor
Manufacturing
Marital Status
Population and Housing
Poverty
Prices and Inflation
Finance and Employment
Retail and Wholesale
Historical Population

The Census Bureau maintains detailed statistics on all these demographic categories.

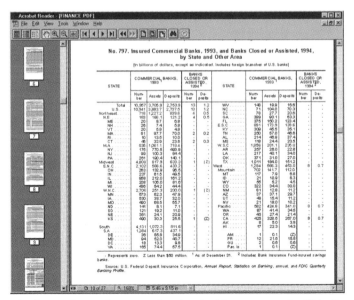

The Census Bureau has created an invaluable resource at its Web site by making huge amounts of data available at little or no cost. Perhaps more than any other government agency, the Bureau has recognized the power of the Internet to serve its constituency.

Business establishment and summary data

Just as massive storehouses of information about individuals and groups have been collected for use in marketing, so too is information maintained on business entities.

Business location files contain the exact whereabouts of virtually every business enterprise. They are generally sold according to Standard Industry Classification (SIC) codes, which group businesses by the types of goods and services they provide. These files allow business-to-business marketers to plot strategy on a very precise scale.

Business summary data totals the number of businesses in each ZIP Code according to SIC code. In addition to listing the number of businesses in an area, these files also summarize total sales volume by SIC code.

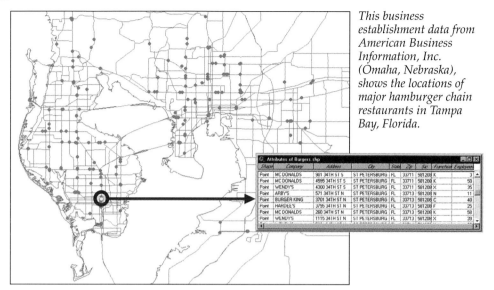

This business establishment data from American Business Information, Inc. (Omaha, Nebraska), shows the locations of major hamburger chain restaurants in Tampa Bay, Florida.

Business-Facts On-CD *from Equifax National Decision Systems (San Diego, California) provides detailed summaries of business data by SIC code, number of employees, and revenue.*

ATTRIBUTE DATA

Segmentation data

Lifestyle segmentation, or clustering, systems classify all U.S. households into unique market segments. Each segment comprises households that share common purchasing patterns, financial behavior, and needs for products and services.

One such system is the *PRIZM®* database from Claritas, Inc. (Ithaca, New York), that was used to create the map of Seattle, Washington, below. By identifying concentrations of lifestyle and behavior patterns, businesses can target their best prospects, and not misdirect advertising and marketing resources.

As the table for census tract 0034.00 suggests, most areas contain just a handful of the sixty-two possible household classifications. Of the 1,638 households found in this tract, 70 percent (1,132) are classified as "Urban Achievers," and 20 percent (339) as "Money & Brains."

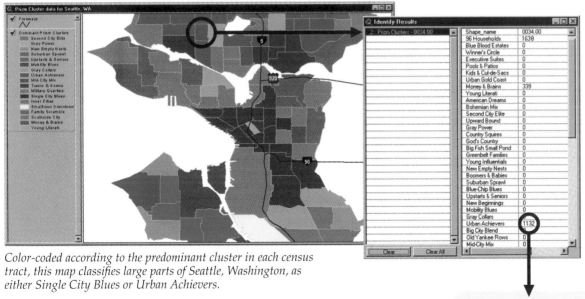

Color-coded according to the predominant cluster in each census tract, this map classifies large parts of Seattle, Washington, as either Single City Blues or Urban Achievers.

Urban Achievers:

Often found near urban, public universities, these neighborhoods are ethnically diverse with a bimodal, young/old age profile. Single students mix with professionals in business, finance, and public service. Age groups: 25–34, 65+. Dominant: White, Asian, and Hispanic.

Environmental Systems Research Institute, Inc.

Consumer potential data

Another useful type of attribute data for businesses is consumer potential data (also known as consumer demand data).

Using statistics from public agencies that collect sales tax data, consumer potential databases give detailed breakdowns of how much people spend on various goods and services. This map of census block groups in Riverside County, California, shows which areas will buy the most gasoline, and which the least, during the current year. The data comes from ESRI's *MarketPac-Express* CD.

Consumer potential data is routinely used by site selection experts to help them figure out the best places to locate new businesses.

Attributes of 1996 Gas Consumption Estimates

Shape	Id	Block Group Name	Area	Annual Gasoline Consumption
Polygon	060650301001	301.001	0.20	284531
Polygon	060650301002	301.002	0.15	349019
Polygon	060650301003	301.003	0.16	165076
Polygon	060650301004	301.004	0.36	318796
Polygon	060650301005	301.005	0.39	1126631
Polygon	060650301009	301.009	0.54	269441
Polygon	060650302001	302.001	0.84	693525
Polygon	060650302002	302.002	0.13	411712
Polygon	060650302003	302.003	0.12	598879
Polygon	060650302004	302.004	0.19	584948
Polygon	060650302009	302.009	0.81	246436

1996 gasoline consumption estimates for western Riverside County. The dark blue areas, showing the highest rates of consumption, tend to be near major freeways and highways.

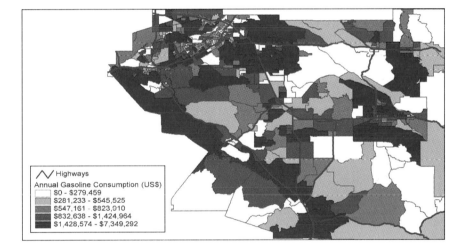

Highways

Annual Gasoline Consumption (US$)
- $0 - $279,459
- $281,233 - $545,525
- $547,161 - $823,910
- $832,638 - $1,424,964
- $1,428,574 - $7,349,292

Financial services data

Financial services data is information about people and their money. This data is used by banks and other financial institutions to aim marketing campaigns at the right people.

The two maps on this page were created with the Claritas (Ithaca, New York) *Financial Clout* database for Orange County, California. In addition to things like total bank deposits and average number of credit cards per household, this database includes hundreds of other variables covering everything from Keough and 401(k) participants to auto loans and home mortgage balances. In fact, financial services data sets are among the most detailed of all consumer databases on the market.

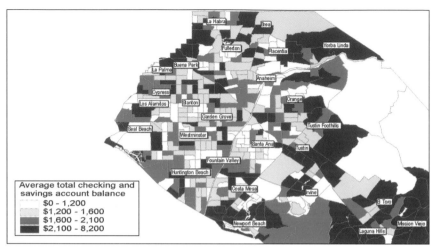

This map displays average total bank deposits (savings and checking) for census tracts in Orange County, California. Pockets of wealth are found in the beach and rural hillside communities.

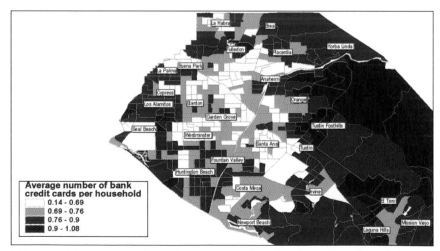

This map of the same area shows the average number of credit cards per household.

Bank branch data

Another type of financial data relates to bank branch locations. Given the dynamic nature of the banking industry, these databases must be monitored and updated frequently to be useful marketing tools.

Bank attribute information can reveal all sorts of things about individual branch locations, including current-year deposits, previous-year deposits, date established, date acquired by another bank, and so on. In the example below, the points are scaled to represent the total deposits held by each bank.

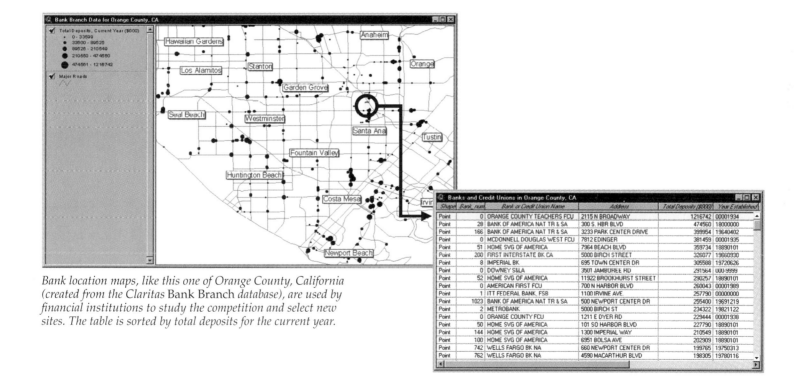

Bank location maps, like this one of Orange County, California (created from the Claritas Bank Branch *database), are used by financial institutions to study the competition and select new sites. The table is sorted by total deposits for the current year.*

Insurance risk data

Insurance risk data profiles the geo-graphical and historical patterns of such natural menaces as hurricanes, earthquakes, hailstorms, wind-storms, and tornados. It is useful to insurance underwriters doing risk assessments, as well as to emergency planners and others.

The map of Connecticut, at right, shows hurricane tracks color-coded by twenty-five-year increments. Though historical activity is spread pretty evenly across the state, almost all of the hurricanes of the last twenty-five years (the blue lines) have passed through the high-value Bridgeport-Hartford corridor. This might have a bearing, for instance, on insurance rates charged to home owners in the area.

Insurance companies doing GIS analysis rely on databases like the HurricaneInfo *package from On Target Mapping (Pittsburgh, Pennsylvania).*

Health care data

Health care consumer demand data, like the sample here from HealthDemographics (San Diego, California), is useful in planning resource allocation and in selecting locations for care centers, clinics, retirement homes, and so on. Hospitals and other providers can use these data sets to profile their patient base, project facility use and caseloads, and analyze service areas.

Other health data sets include physician point locations and files for major diagnostic categories.

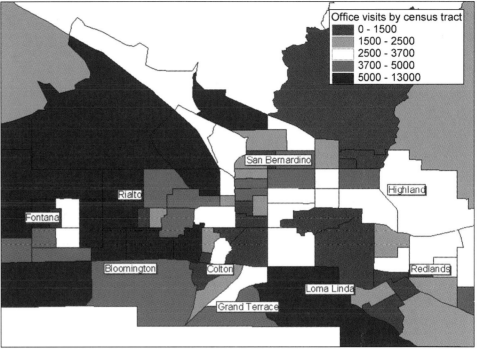

This map shows the number of pediatric physician office visits by census tract for southwestern San Bernardino County, California.

The ArcData Publishing Program

ArcData on the Web

The ArcData℠ Publishing Program was established by ESRI in 1991 to make high-quality data sets available for use with ESRI geographic information system software. Data publishers who are certified members of the program have ensured that their data is fully compatible with ESRI products.

The *ArcData Catalog* (available in hard copy or online) offers hundreds of map files containing a wide variety of spatial and attribute data. Refer to ESRI's ArcData Web page at www.esri.com/data for links to the home pages of ArcData publishers as well as other information that will help you find the data you need.

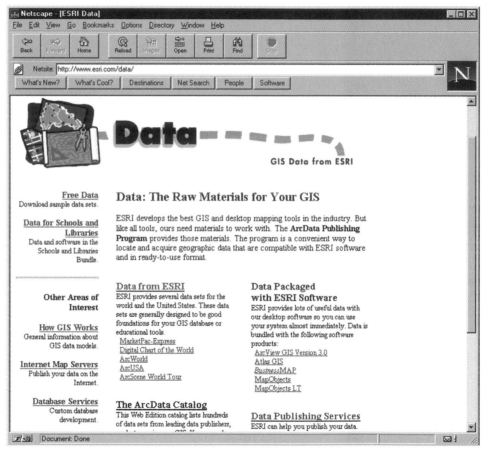

ESRI's ArcData *program can help you find the data you need for virtually any GIS application.*

The data that comes with ArcView GIS

ArcView GIS ships with over a gigabyte of ready-to-use data. For many applications, you may not need to look any further. These map files are in vector format (except for the one image) and come with selected attribute data.

Hamburger franchises: Contains nationwide locations for the franchises of six major hamburger chains.

Census tracts: Contains census tracts for all fifty states and the District of Columbia.

National highways: Contains the nation's principal arterial highway system and other routes.

National interstates: Contains urban and rural interstate routes.

Landmarks: Contains nationwide locations for common landmarks, including airports, cemeteries, parks, and educational facilities.

Major roads: Contains interstate, federal, and state highways and other major thoroughfares within the United States.

Metropolitan Statistical Areas: Contains Metropolitan Statistical Areas for the United States.

Places: Contains locations for all populated places in the United States.

States and counties: Contains boundaries for all fifty states and the District of Columbia, and all U.S. counties.

Topographic relief image: An image of North America in TIFF format.

Plant nurseries, miniature golf establishments, and theaters: Contains nationwide locations for these businesses.

Three-digit ZIP Codes: Contains three-digit ZIP Code boundaries for all fifty states and the District of Columbia.

Five-digit ZIP Codes: Contains five-digit ZIP Code boundaries for all fifty states and the District of Columbia.

Countries: Contains boundaries for 258 countries of the world, including those created from the former Soviet Union, Yugoslavia, and Czechoslovakia.

States and provinces: Contains state, province, and other primary administrative boundaries for the countries of the world.

What's next?

By now, if you've already read through all the case studies and this data chapter, you may be feeling a bit overwhelmed by all this new material. Remember, the people using GIS in business are people just like you, without special training. Of course, GIS introduces some new concepts, so there is a learning curve associated with it, but it is also very exciting technology and the benefits are well worth the effort it takes to become proficient.

And don't tell your boss, but GIS also happens to be a whole lot of fun. So as you begin your own GIS projects, just remember to relax and enjoy yourself.

The CD–ROM

The CD–ROM included with this book, while not directly integrated with the content of the text, provides a useful introduction to the basics of actually using ArcView GIS. The CD is easy to install, and includes a working copy of the software with which to complete the exercises or just experiment.

Additional resources

Here are some excellent resources to help expand your GIS knowledge:

Getting to Know ArcView GIS from ESRI is the definitive how-to text. Order it online at *www.esri.com/base/store.*

The *ArcData Catalog* is a comprehensive description of ESRI-software-compatible data.

User guides and online documentation included with ArcView GIS, ArcView Spatial Analyst, and ArcView Network Analyst will answer even the toughest questions.

1-800-GIS-XPRT (447-9778) is ESRI's toll-free information line that works from anywhere in the United States.

ArcView-L is an Internet discussion group where ArcView GIS users answer each other's questions and discuss how to do things in ArcView.

www.esri.com is the starting place for accessing all of ESRI's Internet resources.

Business Geographics is a national magazine focusing on GIS in business. For information, contact *GIS World*, Fort Collins, Colorado.

To contact the author directly, send e-mail to *charder@esri.com.* To participate in a discussion forum on this book, link to the ESRI book conferences at *www.esri.com/esribooks.*

G l o s s a r y

ARC/INFO   A GIS software package from ESRI that runs on UNIX® workstations and Windows NT. Map files created with ARC/INFO software may be used in ArcView GIS.

ArcView Internet Map Server   An ArcView GIS extension that supports live mapping and GIS applications on the World Wide Web.

ArcView Network Analyst   An ArcView GIS extension that supports network analysis, including finding best routes, nearest facilities, and facility service areas.

ArcView Spatial Analyst   An ArcView GIS extension that supports spatial and statistical analysis of raster data and the integrated use of raster and vector data.

attribute   A piece of information describing a map feature. The attributes of a ZIP Code, for example, might include its area, population, and average per capita income. Attribute data is one of the two main types of data in a GIS (the other being spatial data).

Automated Vehicle Location (AVL)   An integrated system using GPS, GIS, and communications technology to track the location and movement of vehicles in real time.

Avenue   The object-oriented programming language that comes with ArcView GIS. The Avenue™ language provides tools for customizing ArcView GIS and developing applications.

buffer	A zone around a map feature measured in units of distance or time. For example, a store's fifteen-minute drive-time buffer defines the area in which drivers can reach the store in fifteen minutes or less.
census block	The smallest geographical unit for which the U.S. Census Bureau collects and tabulates decennial census information. Census blocks are bounded on all sides by visible features (such as streets) or nonvisible features (such as township lines). To protect privacy, a minimum of demographic information is reported at this level.
census block group	A combination of census blocks that is a subdivision of a census tract. The block group is the smallest unit for which the Census Bureau reports a full range of demographic statistics.
census tract	A small, relatively permanent statistical subdivision of a county. Census tract boundaries normally follow visible features, but may follow governmental unit boundaries or other nonvisible features. A census tract may contain anywhere between 2,500 and 8,000 people.
chart	A graphic representation of data values. ArcView GIS supports six chart types: column, bar, pie, area, line, and x,y scatter. Two of these (column and pie) can be used as symbols in ArcView maps.
classification	A scheme for dividing map features into a specified number of classes according to selected attribute values. Sales territories, for example, might be divided into five classes according to the number of accounts they contain. Each class is then assigned a unique symbol to create a thematic map.

Environmental Systems Research Institute, Inc.

continuous surface map A map representing a geographic phenomenon that lacks definite boundaries and has variable values across a surface (for example, elevation or population density). Continuous surface maps are created from raster data.

dBASE file A file format native to dBASE data management software. ArcView GIS can read, create, and export tables in dBASE format.

demographics The statistical characteristics of a population (for example, income, education, race, and home ownership).

desktop GIS A geographic information system, such as ArcView GIS, that runs on a personal computer.

digitizing The process of electronically tracing features on a paper map to convert them to features in a digital map file. Accomplished with a special piece of computer hardware called a *digitizing tablet.*

dot density map A map in which dots are used to represent the density of an attribute (for instance, population).

extension An optional ArcView GIS module that performs a specialized function. ArcView Network Analyst, ArcView Spatial Analyst, and ArcView Internet Map Server are a few of the many ArcView software extensions.

feature A map representation of a geographic object. Store sites, customer locations, streets, census tracts, and ZIP Codes are examples of map features. Features are drawn as points, lines, and polygons in ArcView GIS.

| geocoding | The process of converting tabular location data (for instance, a database of customer addresses) into accurately placed features in a map file. ArcView GIS has built-in geocoding capabilities. |

| geographic information system (GIS) | A configuration of computer hardware and software that stores, displays, and analyzes geographic data. |

| global positioning system (GPS) | A radio-navigation technology that uses satellite signals to calculate the position of objects on the earth's surface, along with their speed and direction. |

| image data | One of the three types of spatial data in a GIS (the others being vector and raster data). Photographs taken from satellites and airplanes are examples of image data. |

| Internet | A decentralized computer network linking tens of thousands of smaller networks and accessed by more than 30 million users worldwide. Users connected to the Internet can send and receive e-mail, download files, view multimedia content on the World Wide Web, and run software applications stored on remote computers. |

| layer | A set of related map features and attributes, stored as a unique file in a geographic database. A GIS can display multiple layers (for instance, counties, roads, and hamburger stands) at the same time. |

| layout | In ArcView GIS, a presentation document incorporating maps, charts, tables, text, and images. |

Environmental Systems Research Institute, Inc.

legend A list of the symbols appearing on a map; a legend includes a sample of each symbol as well as text that explains the symbol's meaning.

map file A computer file containing spatial and attribute information for a set of geographic objects.

map scale The relationship between the dimensions of features on a map and the geographic objects they represent on the earth, commonly expressed as a ratio or fraction. A map scale of 1:100,000 means that one unit of measure on the map equals 100,000 of the same unit on the earth.

Metropolitan Statistical Area (MSA) An urbanized area as defined by the U.S. Office of Management and Budget, consisting of a core area containing a large population nucleus, together with adjacent communities having a high degree of economic and social integration with that core. Normally, an MSA includes at least one city of 50,000 or more inhabitants, or an urbanized area of at least 50,000 inhabitants and a total metropolitan population of at least 100,000.

raster data One of the three types of spatial data in a GIS (the others being vector and image data). Raster data represents geographic space as a matrix of cells; map features are defined by numeric values assigned to the cells.

script In ArcView GIS, a program written in the Avenue scripting language.

service area The area served by a given facility, specified in units of distance or time.

spatial analysis The determination of the spatial relationships between geographic objects, such as the distance between them or the extent to which they overlap.

spatial data
One of the two main types of data in a GIS (the other being attribute data). Spatial data represents the shape, location, or appearance of geographic objects. It can be in vector, raster, or image format.

symbol
A particular graphic element or icon (defined by some combination of shape, size, color, angle, outline, and fill pattern) used to draw a map feature. An airport, for example, might be represented by an icon of a blue airplane. ArcView GIS comes with hundreds of symbols to choose from; additional symbols can be created from fonts or imported from images.

symbology
The aspect of map design dealing with the choice of symbols, colors, and text fonts.

thematic map
A map that symbolizes features according to a particular attribute. Examples are a map displaying businesses as dots of different sizes according to number of employees, and a map displaying census tracts in different colors according to median household income.

TIGER
The U.S. Census Bureau's digital geographic database. (TIGER is an acronym for Topographically Integrated Geographic Encoding and Referencing.) The TIGER database contains complete coverage for the United States and its territories. It defines the location and relationship of streets, rivers, railroads, and other features to each other and to the numerous geographic entities (such as census tracts) for which the Census Bureau tabulates data.

topographic relief map
A graphic representation of differences in the level of the earth's surface.

trade area
The region from which a store derives a certain percentage of its business.

Environmental Systems Research Institute, Inc.

vector data   One of the three types of spatial data in a GIS (the others being raster and image data). Vector data represents geographic objects as points, lines, or polygons.

World Wide Web   A client/server system for distributing and accessing multimedia documents on the Internet. Documents on the World Wide Web are formatted in a special language called HTML (HyperText Markup Language) that supports links to other documents.